Advance praise for Don Greene's Audition Success

"Audition Success is a must read for all musicians seeking professional careers."

Julie Landsman, Principal Horn, Metropolitan Opera Orchestra.
Faculty, The Juilliard School

Testimonials from Don Greene's former students

"Dr. Greene is a wonderful teacher. His words of wisdom are always insightful and illuminating. *Audition Success* really opened my eyes to a new way of auditioning and music making. It's an indispensable tool for any musician."

Tom Sherwood, Principal Percussionist,
Atlanta Symphony Orchestra

"Before working with Dr. Greene, I was too often preoccupied with the 'what-if's' while I was playing. However, through his methods of centering and visualization, among others, my concentration and sense of focus has since drastically improved my performance on many levels. This book is a 'must-have' for anyone who wants to beat their own mind games!"

Julia Pilant, Principal Horn, Syracuse Symphony

Also by Don Greene, Ph.D.
Fight Your Fear and Win

Audition Success

An Olympic Sports Psychologist
Teaches Performing Artists
How to Win

Don Greene, Ph.D.

ROUTLEDGE
New York

Published in 2001 by
Routledge
29 West 35th Street
New York, NY 10001

Routledge is an imprint of the Taylor & Francis Group

Printed in the United States of America on acid-free paper
Design and typography: Jack Donner

Library of Congress Cataloging-in-Publication Data is available from
the Library of Congress

ISBN: 0-87830-121-6

Contents

Foreword   vii

Introduction   1

1   *The Profiles*   9
Eighty Miles per Hour
Brian Meets Bob

2   *Process Cues*   25
Breathe
A Training Diary

3   *Centering*   39
Ninety Miles per Hour
Seamless

4   *From Your Center*   57
The Hub of the Wheel
Warm Air and Float

5   *Getting Better*   77
    Sing It at a Seven
    Just "Post-it"

6   *Courage*   95
    Optimal Performance
    Put Yourself on the Spot

7   *New Cues*   115
    Flow
    Clean and Easy

8   *Getting Close*   131
    Trust
    Normal Fears and Doubts

9   *On Location*   149
    Back to the Hub

10 *New Things*   153
    The Dress
    The New Horn

11 *Other Energy*   159
    It Just Kicked In

    Epilogue   165

    Centering Instructions   167

Foreword

Most of us who are performers realize that mental preparation and focus have a significant effect on our performance. However, skills like these are rarely taught. Dr. Don Greene teaches these skills and shows instrumentalists and singers how to use and refine them, as they would any other aspect of their technique.

In addition to my career as a concert pianist and conductor, I have taught piano and coached singers for over twenty years. After seeing Dr. Greene's work with members of the Florida Philharmonic, the Miami Opera, and the Lake George Opera Festival, I can honestly say that his ability to enhance performance skills is amazing.

His work with professional and Olympic athletes for the last ten years has made him a leading expert in optimizing physical coordination with acute focus. His more recent work with performing artists has given him a deep understanding of the issues that are crucial to us in rehearsals, auditions, and important performances.

Don's enthusiasm, enjoyment of the artists with whom he works, and genuine love of music make him a tremendous asset to both professional and aspiring artists. Our singers and instrumentalists have gained confidence and skills that they learned from working with him. I'm sure you'll find the same to be true.

Joe Illick

Introduction

One warm summer evening in Colorado a few years ago, I pulled into my garage after conducting a grueling yet rewarding three-day golf clinic in Denver. I was glad to be home. The clinic had gone extremely well. The participants had gone away with more confidence, better focus, and a more positive approach to playing the game, a transformation that never ceases to thrill me. The entire field of sports psychology had captured my interest in the late seventies, which led to a rewarding career working with Olympic and professional athletes in sports ranging from platform diving to Grand Prix driving.

With such a dynamic profession that continued to teach me something new every day, I had little idea of what lay beyond the world of competitive sports. In fact, it was a recreational golfer who would ultimately lead me to my next big challenge in a world I knew nothing about—classical music.

The phone began ringing as soon as I unlocked my front door. I raced to grab the receiver before my machine picked it up. The guy on the other end of the line was inquiring about my availability for an individual session. In addition to being an avid golfer, he was also a bassist playing in the Vail summer concert series. Could I help him lower his handicap a few strokes in less than an hour? "Sure," I replied. "In return for a bass lesson or two." I smiled, never one to pass up a new opportunity. We agreed to get together the next morning at the local golf course.

I met Ed on the putting green and soon found out that he was really a good golfer, but he was struggling with his putting. I asked him about his preshot routine for his putting—what he was doing in the last twenty to thirty seconds before he hit his putt. I asked him to show me what he normally did when he was playing, from reading the break of the green, to taking practice strokes, to hitting the putt. But seeing what he was doing raised more questions than it answered. What did he do under different circumstances? With longer putts? In more critical situations?

We went out and played nine holes. I saw him hit a lot of good shots and I also noticed certain things he was doing that were not helpful. When we had finished playing, I told Ed that I was impressed by his swing and that I had some thoughts about his putting routine. However, I first needed more information before I could make any recommendations. I asked Ed to complete a questionnaire, a sports psychology survey, which asks athletes how they perform certain skills under pressure. After a computer had tallied his responses, it would produce an individual profile of what he already did well and where he needed the most improvement.

He told me that he would take the survey, but asked if I had any ideas on what he could do right away to improve his performance. I told him that I wouldn't know until I saw his profile, and that I hadn't had my bass lesson yet. He said that he didn't like transporting his stand-up bass all over town. Would I mind coming backstage for the lesson after the concert that evening? He would leave my ticket at the "Will Call" desk and he would have the survey done by then.

The concert that night was great; so was the bass lesson. I wasn't. I had taken some electric guitar lessons, but that was years ago, and this was very different. Ed was obviously an excellent teacher, but it really hurt my fingers to hold the thick steel strings down for any length of time. I soon asked for mercy. No, I couldn't learn to play the bass in less than an hour, but I was certain we could make significant improvements in his golf game, or at least his putting.

We met in the clubhouse the next morning and went over his computerized profile. We found several issues related to his putting difficulties: he wasn't getting a good feel for the length of the putt before addressing it; he tended to stand over the ball too long before he stroked it. Ed was thinking too much before he ever started his putting motion, and that caused him to be less than totally focused on making the putt.

We went out to the putting green and worked on his putting routine. It was fairly standard stuff in my practice. An hour later, after he had become comfortable with the changes I suggested, we went out and played another nine holes. This time, the results were very different. Ed had 35 putts for the first nine holes we played; for the second nine he had only 31. If he could do that on a regular basis, he really would lower his handicap.

After we were done, Ed said that what we had done with his golf game applied to symphony musicians—that most of the performance issues were similar to the ones that musicians dealt with every day. I asked for his help rewriting my athletes' survey in musicians' terms. Instead of asking athletes if they were nervous before a competition, for example, we would ask artists how they felt before an audition.

That fall, Ed arranged for me to come to the Syracuse Symphony, where he is the Principal Bass, and offer what was now the performing artists' survey to his fellow musicians. The conductor gave me two minutes to address the entire orchestra before a rehearsal. I admitted that I didn't have any experience working with performing artists, but invited them to take the survey anyway. I would have their computer printouts the following day, and we could start to discuss their profiles then. About forty musicians chose to participate.

I met the next day with those forty musicians and went over their profiles. It led to a fascinating session about the similarities between high-level sports and music. We met the following day, when about sixty musicians showed up. The final day, almost the entire orchestra came to the session. Before we finished, I asked them for their written comments and critique.

The concert master wrote: "Great work . . . even a hint of negativity would sabotage the many wonderful things you shared with us." The principal trumpet player wrote that it increased his awareness and desire to improve, and that it "reaffirmed my belief in life being a journey, not a destination." Another one of the principals described our two sessions as "practical information . . . an organized approach to concentration, motivation and readiness to play one's best."

At the concert that evening, I was hanging out backstage during the first movement. One of the principals asked if we could talk, saying that he didn't have a part until the second movement. We went to a rehearsal room and sat down. He told me that he opened the second movement with a solo that tormented him. He had tried everything under the sun to help him deal with his anxiety, but he never knew if he would hit it or have another painful experience. It was destroying his otherwise happy, well-adjusted life.

I never knew that it could be that way with musicians; I thought they just sat there and played. Listening to this talented and proud man explain his ordeal touched me. I knew there were sports psychology techniques that could help him, but there wasn't enough time to teach him in these final minutes before he went on. All I could do was offer some words of encouragement. Before leaving Syracuse, Ed and I revised the survey to address better the real challenges that he and his colleagues faced on a regular basis.

That summer, I addressed the Florida Philharmonic before

a rehearsal. This time, I was given three minutes, not two, to convince skeptical musicians to complete the survey and attend a feedback session on their individual profiles, and that sports psychology could help them do better what they already did well. One of musicians who chose to participate was a trombonist. He was preparing for an audition with the San Francisco Symphony Orchestra and really wanted to win the job. After we went through his profile, we agreed to start working together. We met once or twice a week for two months.

We tried all sorts of things, both old and new. He was doing better and better every week. By the time he left for the audition, he was prepared, confident, and ready to win. He played well through the first series of excerpts, and continued playing well into the second. Then suddenly, his mouth went dry. He'd become dehydrated from his cross-country red-eye flight the night before. It was very important for him to have enough moisture in his mouth when he was playing. He knew immediately that that was it—he was done.

I should have thought to ask him about his travel arrangements, but we never discussed them. I know how critical it is for athletes to factor in the negative effects of jet lag on performance, but I hadn't asked. We both felt terrible.

That winter, I went back to the Syracuse Symphony to do a follow-up visit. It was great to see everyone again. They took the revised survey and we talked about what we'd learned since we'd last been together. After the two group sessions, I scheduled half-hour sessions with individual musicians to discuss their profiles.

One of these was Brian, a 35-year-old horn player I had met during my previous visit. He told me that he was starting to prepare for an important audition with the Houston Symphony. Brian mentioned that he had experienced some difficulties in recent auditions and asked for my assistance. We agreed to work together over the phone after I got back home.

That summer, I was invited to the Lake George Opera

Festival to work with the apprentice artists. They were just about to start the final week of rehearsals for *Rigoletto*, which was opening in five days. I tried to schedule at least one session with each of the singers during their upcoming busy week.

I met the following day with Veronica, a 28-year-old mezzo-soprano. She had a leading role in *Rigoletto* and another part in *Gianni Schicchi*. She was facing a challenging week of rehearsals and performances. I was about to have one of the most incredible weeks of my life, being around a group of talented performers in their final preparation. I learned a great deal by observing the rehearsals, but it was the individual sessions, one on one with different singers, where I really started to appreciate the struggles that these artists faced in their careers.

Through Brian and Veronica I will show you a different approach to stressful performance situations. As I help them prepare for their auditions, they'll progress through three stages. These are the same phases that my clients go through in preparing for recitals, solos, important concerts, and auditions. In the first stage, I assess their performance strengths and weaknesses, and teach them Centering to focus and control their energy. The second stage includes using tools such as mental rehearsal, process cues, and simulation training. The final phase puts it all together, with artists forming a positive outlook to approaching stressful performances, when they're able to trust their talent, training and, most important, themselves.

Although this approach may be considered a means to alleviate performance anxiety, I don't see it that way. I do not like the term performance anxiety. Putting a label on something as normal as the energy which accompanies most stressful circumstances is not helpful. It somehow makes what highly functioning individuals experience before and during live performances wrong, as if it were a disease. It may be uncomfortable until one learns what to do with it, but it's not a disease. Thinking that it's wrong and needs to be suppressed can make it more of a problem than need be.

The solution is to interpret the myriad of symptoms that

accompany high-stress situations (racing heart, perspiration, butterflies, clammy hands, and so on) not only as normal but to be expected and accepted. Rather than feeling those things and thinking "Oh, no, why now? Now I'm going to mess up," the idea is to feel that same energy and realize "I know this is important, the adrenaline's kicked in, my body's gearing up, I'm getting ready for an energized performance."

This will *not* make those symptoms go away, but it will help you use the energy in a far more productive way. Rather than trying to suppress it, the goal is to regulate and use that energy for more focused, exciting, and powerful performances. That's what gets standing ovations, not cautious, low energy renditions that bore the audience. It's also what wins auditions. In the time since I worked with Veronica and Brian, my clients have won over seventy professional orchestral and opera auditions.

Throughout the book, I will strive to emphasize several key concepts. These are: learning how to Center effectively; doing simulation training; using appropriate process cues; the concept of optimal performance versus trying to be perfect; keeping thoughts positive or being mentally quiet; the need for courage; developing a preperformance routine; and learning to trust yourself.

The bottom line is that this is a better way to approach high-pressure situations: being positive versus negative, being focused versus scattered, and using that energy versus freaking out. I seek to change not only your paradigm of how to approach auditions and important performances, but also your experience of them, so they become less of a dread and more enjoyable, exciting, and *better*. Imagine that!

What follows are the taped conversations with Brian and Veronica, with their express consent. They are as close to verbatim as readability allows. I hope that you learn and profit from their journeys.

CHAPTER ONE

The Profiles

EIGHTY MILES PER HOUR

Veronica and I met in a conference room at the high school where they were conducting the final rehearsals of *Rigoletto*. She had already completed the survey, so I brought her profile with me. I asked her what she thought we were going to do during our session. She laughed.

"I have no idea."

Do you have any expectations?

"You know, I don't even think I have any expectations. I'm just very curious."

That's good. So please tell me about your background and how you got started in music.

"Umm. . . . I grew up in New England and I studied piano and theater in high school. In college at New York University, I spent my first year at the Tisch School of Arts studying drama. But I wasn't happy, so I went to France for my sophomore year.

The University of Paris has a year-long course for foreign students in French history and culture. So I did that, and I actually studied piano in Paris. Then I came back and I switched . . . is this too much detail?"

No, this is great.

"I switched my major to French. By my senior year at NYU, I started taking voice lessons for fun. I didn't really expect anything from it, but I knew I had always liked to sing. But the woman I studied with was very encouraging and gave me tickets to the opera. I really, really liked it a lot because it had all the elements of things that I had always loved, languages, theater and music, all in one. Plus, I seemed to have a natural ability to do it."

Were those lessons you took regular voice lessons or opera lessons?

"It was all classical music and opera; that was her interest. I didn't even know anything about opera when I started. I just liked to sing. I was with her about a year, and I auditioned for a master's program at the Manhattan School of Music. It was the Conservatory, and I was accepted. My master's degree took three years because I had no musical education up until that point. So I just got through that, and then after I graduated, I started auditioning for music apprentice–type programs and studying all along . . . and that's been for the last year and a half."

Well thanks. Would you like to look at your profile?

"This is the scary part, I think."

There's nothing to fear. And besides, there's a number of really good things on your profile.

"That's reassuring!"

Learning more about Veronica's journey into music

reinforced what her profile would show as strengths, particularly her motivation and strong commitment to music. She was a strong-willed, enthusiastic performer who loved what she was doing, but often got caught up in the excitement of performing. I began to take her through the different categories in order to validate her profile.

First of all, your Intrinsic Motivation is very high. That's wonderful!

"What does that mean?"

It means that your prime motivation is from within and that you're driven as a performer. It would appear that you're doing it for your own reasons, your own pride and the satisfaction of performing your best.

"That's true, I've always been self-motivated."

Your Commitment is also in the high range. That suggests that you are very invested in your career and success.

"So far this all seems very positive, but I know I'm not perfect. Is a high score always good?

Not necessarily. In fact, the next couple of scores, which are relatively high, may reveal what is hindering you in performances. Let's find out what your profile says about your Activation levels.

"My what?"

Your Activation or energy levels. They're a combination of your physical and mental energies. They're measured before you go out on stage and while you're rehearsing, performing, or auditioning. All of those scores are high; that means you're probably experiencing a lot of adrenaline and anxiety before and during live performances. It says you have a high "rev rate" that you are highly activated, with lots of energy. You probably come into rehearsals or performances really 'up.' . . .

"Yes, my heart always seems to be racing just before I have to perform."

... and I see that your Optimal Activation is very high.

"What's that mean?"

It means you sing your best when you're 'up.' Think of when you're singing really well. You sing your best, or optimally, when you're at a very high energy level, as if you were going 80 miles per hour. Right?

"Yeah!" Veronica laughed. "You're not kidding."

You're running your engine at a high rate of speed all the time. That can be draining, and if you go a little past that already high level of 80, then you're into redline. You sing your best at a high energy level. So if you're already up and if something unexpected happens, you're over the line, your cup just overflowed ... and that's when you could get into trouble.

"That tends to happen a lot. But what can I do about it?"

We're getting to that. [She nodded.] That's good, but you have trouble doing the reverse. Your score of average for Ability to Deactivate means that at times you may have trouble bringing your energy level or anxiety down, especially when it gets way too high. So when you need to relax....

"That's really hard for me."

That's my concern with you running at an 80. If something else happens and you hit an 85, you might not be able to bring it down. And knowing that, in itself, will cause your anxiety to go even higher.

"Oh God. I'm going to explode."

But you can learn how to control that energy.

"Good. I just get so uptight about it all."

We'll come back to that. Your Fear of Failure score is low. This fear is fueling your anxiety and saying, 'I'm not sure how it's going to go.' and 'What if I do this wrong?' Just more fuel for your quick-running engine. You just dumped in some nitro fuel.

"Oh no!" She laughed.

Is it accurate?

"Yes, that's exactly what it feels like."

Your Mental Quiet score is also low. That means you're thinking too much or too fast. And if you're thinking about what could go wrong, it's going to keep your activation levels high. That extra thinking and worrying is overdriving your revved-up engine. You can see how many of these results are intertwined.

"Yeah. Oh, wow."

Your Performance Under Pressure score is in the average range. It means that sometimes you perform well under pressure and sometimes you don't. In a performance situation, when you're at an 'up' and positive 80 and feeling good, then you do well. But when you cross that line and get to 85 or 90, then you don't perform as well as you can.

Veronica nodded. "That makes sense."

Your Self-Talk score is average and says that sometimes you stay positive and sometimes you beat yourself up or chew yourself out. Sometimes you're positive and encouraging, sometimes you're self-critical. It probably depends on the situation.

"Staying positive is a new thing for me. I've only been able to do it for the last six months or so."

How?

"Well, I was working with this one coach. He believed that where you were wasn't important. It's just great to be doing what you're doing, that you're up and going forward. He just had a great attitude."

Did those ideas feel comfortable?

"Yeah. They felt really comfortable, and so I got used to talking to myself that way. Then one time at an audition, I had this experience where I was so scared that I was shaking. I couldn't even breathe. So I said to myself, 'You know, you must be a very brave person to do this. Even though you're so scared, you're still doing it.' And that's when it really started. Just being able to see how scared I was and yet do it anyway, no matter how it would come out. Just getting up there and doing it deserves . . . I don't know . . . something."

I agree.

"That didn't make me feel any less nervous necessarily, it just made me less down on myself."

It took the nervous edge off, but it left you with the same physiological symptoms.

"Right . . . and then my fear of failure . . . but there are other voices . . . it's like millions of voices saying different things. . . ."

We'll get to that. But what you've already done is what you need to learn to do even better. I just want to support your continuing learning of it, because it's very critical for you to continue the process. But it hinges around how you talk to yourself and whether you're positive or negative with your self-talk. We'll get back to that later. Now, your score on Ability to Recover is high. That's wonderful! It means that if you do make a mistake, you can recover and come back; it doesn't devastate you. You can bounce back quickly.

"That's never been difficult for me. I just say, 'OK' and go on."

Your Commitment score is very high. That tells me that singing is very important in your life.

"Yes!"

Your Self-Confidence score is in the average range. That's tied to your self-talk, or the way you talk to yourself inside your head. When you beat yourself up verbally, your self-confidence is going to go down. When you stay positive, it goes up. But right now, I need to know if you feel your profile is accurate.

"Yes. It seems right on target."

Good. You have some wonderful stuff, like your motivation, your ability to recover and your commitment. You have some things that have a lot to do with your thinking, that can work either way. You need to learn how to use better the things that have worked for you, and use them more often. So Veronica, do you have any questions?

"I don't think so. It's amazing how well these profiles worked. They really came up with some good insights."

Good. So when do you sing again?

"I might sing at the dress rehearsal tomorrow night, and in the afternoon it's the rehearsal for the other opera."

Would you like to get together tomorrow?

"Sure. How about after the rehearsal?"

Great. I'll see you at the rehearsal hall.

I left Veronica with a lot to think about before our next meeting, particularly her self-talk, the need to stay positive, and her high rev rate. My next student, Brian, provided a vastly different example of a talented musician struggling in certain performances. You will see that not all artists deal with stressful situations in the same way.

BRIAN MEETS BOB

My first meeting with Brian in Syracuse was in one of the backstage dressing rooms at the concert hall. He mentioned that he had recently set up an audition with the Houston Symphony that he wanted very much to win. He needed to play well to do that, but he had an underlying concern that he didn't audition well or play well enough to compete with the very best.

"A few years ago, I was making the finals in auditions for several major orchestras. Now I'm not even getting out of prelims, not to mention ever getting close to actually winning a job. And that concerns me, because I'm playing better than I ever have, and yet in auditions, I'm just not doing it."

Brian, would you please tell me about your background in music?

"Sure. I went to Northwestern. I graduated in the class of '81, so I have a bachelor of music degree. I played with the Louisville Orchestra from 1983 through 1989. I was the third horn. I played a couple of years in the Chicago Civic Orchestra, which is the training orchestra of the Chicago Symphony. Civic's a big deal; you get to play with the CSO, but I never did. Somehow I got passed over a couple times. That's something which I've never really totally gotten over. A small part of me is like, 'How come I never got to do that?' It's always kind of pissed me off a little bit, but playing well is the best revenge. It doesn't exactly hold me back anymore. So I was playing in the Chicago Civic and I was basically just freelancing."

When did you audition for the Louisville orchestra?

"Well, first I auditioned for what's now known as the National Repertory Orchestra. Back then it was called the

CPO, the Colorado Philharmonic Orchestra. It was based in Evergreen, Colorado. It's a training program in the summer, with nine weeks of intense repertoire, and I was one of three principals there. I won the Louisville audition shortly thereafter. But Colorado should definitely be on the resume, because that's a big deal; the CPO and then Louisville. So I was in Louisville from '83 to '89, and in the summers from '85 to '89, I played with the Colorado Music Festival in Boulder. I was playing with players from Chicago and New York and really excellent freelancers. It was a great experience. Eight weeks of just absolutely great music and riding your bike and hiking and illicit romantic affairs . . . it had everything."

I laughed along with him. Brian continued.

"I played second and fourth horn, that was my niche and that's fine; I had a great time. As a matter of fact, that last summer in '89, my best friend and I were roommates and we were first and second horn. That's some of the best playing I've ever done in my career. In '89, after he had gotten principal in Columbus, the third horn position became open. He said, 'I know Brian hates it in Louisville. Let's get him.' So I made a decision to leave a tenured position; I hated it that much. I knew this was probably only going to be a one-year position. So, from '89 to '90, that one season, I played in Columbus. I had the unique experience—I don't recommend it—of having to audition for my own job. If I won the audition, I kept the job I already had. If I didn't win the audition, I lost my job and I'd be out on the street. It was kind of the worst of both worlds. I played an okay audition, but even though they knew who it was, they just couldn't hire me. I didn't make it past the prelims. But nobody won the audition. They didn't choose anyone. I was out on the street. So . . . I switched to a new mouthpiece because I wasn't happy with my setup, and three weeks later I won Syracuse."

Is that what happened? Really? I smiled.

"I was unhappy. I didn't have a great season in Columbus. I was having some playing problems because I had made some huge adjustments and I switched a mouthpiece. I just changed too many variables, including who I was playing with and where I was living. It was just too much for me to handle and I just wasn't playing well. And I didn't play a good audition for Columbus. But I got it together very quickly."

Brian had fallen into a classic pattern when faced with stressful situations. In conjunction with a series of poor performances and auditions, he had lost confidence in his playing. Moving from place to place, alternating mouthpieces on his instrument, and changing ensembles had left him disheartened and unfocused. Fortunately, he was able somehow to pull it all together for the Syracuse audition, but he definitely needed to learn how to do that on a more regular basis.

"At first I joined the Syracuse Orchestra as an assistant utility horn. It was a two year contract. But when the associate horn didn't come back, my colleagues voted unanimously to hire me in his place. They had enough confidence in me, including the music director, that they didn't even make me play a couple of excerpts for them as a formality. I was really pleased by that. So I was happy . . . and the first horn was happy . . . everybody was happy. And then, in the last two seasons, when one of the horn players was getting ready to go to the Atlantic Brass Quintet, I basically filled in on fourth. As a matter of fact, the last two seasons, I was acting fourth horn. It wasn't a change of contract, but I was actually fourth Associate Principal, which nobody does, at least not on a consistent basis. But that's what I was asked to do and that's what I did. I did it very successfully."

When did you start thinking about leaving Syracuse?

Brian then went into his current problem. Apparently, he had continued going to various auditions while at Syracuse, and yet he wasn't making it beyond the prelim in any of them. Despite playing better than ever, he wasn't nailing the big auditions for major symphonies, and he couldn't understand why.

"I wasn't getting out of the prelims and it was really getting frustrating because I knew I was playing better than I had before. Finally, I realized that the reason I wasn't getting out of the prelims was because I wasn't preparing for auditions the proper way. That's why I want to work with you. Whatever had worked back then wasn't working now. I decided that it was time to change the game plan."

Tell me more about your last audition.

"Well, first of all, in the Detroit audition, I had a new horn. I felt comfortable on it, but I still didn't quite make it. I was disappointed that I didn't do better. I have gone by what my old teacher told me a couple of months ago, that I should just do what I've been taught and what I know. I've heard great players, studied with great players, and know everything I need. I just need to trust inside. And I know that I really don't need to go to any other teachers; my tape recorder and I can solve any problems. That's where I'm at."

When is the audition in Houston?

"In about eight weeks. Does that give us enough time?"

Hopefully so. But let's go back to the Detroit audition first. [I wanted to get a better idea of where he was losing his focus.]

"I started preparing intensely three weeks before and I think I burned out. I felt myself ramping down in Detroit. I still played a good audition, but I didn't think I was all primed. The thing about Detroit was that I was in a little warm-up room and the person next to me was blasting. All I did was sit back and say, 'This is the first note of Schubert. This is how I'm going to play it.' So I was able to overcome that crummy little room with someone blasting through the excerpts when I just wanted to sit there and be quiet. Apparently I didn't practice enough, because I had a mistake on the fifth excerpt and one small mistake in a previous excerpt, it wasn't a bad one, but two mistakes and I guess they figured, 'He made two mistakes. It wasn't what we were waiting for. He's out of here.' And that was it."

Do you know what caused that second mistake?

"I'd been playing well. But I got to the fifth excerpt and they had put the wrong part on the stand. So I was just going along and I tried to relax. It was a loud excerpt, and then I felt a little shake in my playing; but I played through it and I thought I was doing fine. The mistake seemed to come out of the blue," he said with a frown.

Five minutes before you went out there, how did you feel?

"Very calm and relaxed. I knew what I had to do. They even gave us the list of the excerpts that we would be playing in the prelims. I just psyched myself up more mentally and physically to start with the Schubert. And that went extremely well. It's a part that I've had difficulty with in the past, but I absolutely nailed it. But for the fifth excerpt, it was the wrong part and I was losing a little bit of focus. I played two wrong notes because I expected to see the second horn part, but they put the fourth part to the Tchaikovsky, which I didn't remember until later. I'd stopped right in the middle of it and they said, 'Thank you.' I think they were going to pull the hook on me anyway. I told the monitor that I would like to do that again. They thought about it for a minute and then said, 'Fine, go ahead.' So I played it again, knowing that this time it had to be better. I started out better, but I still 'chipped' something. They just said, 'Thank you' again. It was a disappointing end to what I had hoped would be a good audition, and what had been going well up until that point."

THE PROFILES • 21

So it was otherwise a good audition?

"Yeah, it had been a good audition. Until that excerpt, I thought I was really on a roll. And I was fully prepared to go on and accept that as just a momentary lapse. But I didn't even get the chance. I wasn't the only one, though. I talked to a number of other musicians who also thought that the prelims were very short. But I guess I just didn't play the way I needed to."

It was evident after listening to Brian that one of his problems was his inability to concentrate. His talent and drive were there in full force, but he kept missing, especially when things took him by surprise. This was understandable—many performers struggle with similar problems—but I needed to see what else was involved. It was time to go over Brian's profile with him. I asked when he had completed the survey.

"I took it right before I left for Detroit. I could imagine myself very well being in an audition, so this ought to be pretty accurate."

Let me ask you, do you feel that you were properly prepared for that audition?

"Pretty much. I started three weeks before. I thought my prep was good, but in hindsight, it wasn't quite good enough. Apparently I didn't practice enough, because I still had a mistake on the fifth excerpt. I guess I could have done a little more mental rehearsal. I think I need to do more of that for Houston."

It's also important for you to start designing the preaudition routine that you're going to use in Houston; one that will take you on stage better prepared to play your best. Your profile should give us some good clues about what should be built into that routine. Are you ready to take a look at it?

"Sure."

There are a number of very positive aspects on your profile.

Your Intrinsic Motivation is strong; you're not distractible by external things; you've got an optimistic outlook, which helps you stay positive. Does that sound accurate?

"It does so far."

Your ability to control your performance energy also looks good.

"I think I have the physical stuff down. I did a good job with that in Detroit. I was mostly relaxed, only a little tense. I could feel a little tension in my shoulders, but I still went out and had no shake. I just got a good breath and played."

That's great. Your Ability to Risk Defeat is low. That means that you have more of a fear of failure than I'd like to see it.

"That doesn't surprise me. In fact, it makes perfect sense."

That's good. I'm also concerned with your own over-thinking; thinking too much about what could go wrong.

"Like, 'What if I lose the count?' I do tend to do that, but I would like to eliminate it if I can. I just don't know how to do that."

One possible solution is to give a name to the voice that brings up the 'what if?' questions.

"So I should imagine a person ... ?"

No, just give it a name.

"Should it be a person from my past or just a made-up name?"

Any name that comes to mind. You can think of him throwing a 'what if' at you, like, 'What if I go into this audition and miss the first note?' Think of that coming into your head.

"OK, so I'm going into the audition and I think, 'What if I bash the first note?' Then what?"

Just tell me the name that you'd associate with that voice, the one saying that to you.

"Hmm. . . . How about Bob?"

Great. Now let's take Bob out of your head and externalize him as the one behind the 'what if?' voice. Think of the things that Bob's been saying to you.

"Alright."

And for every 'what if,' rather than taking it internally and letting it snowball and buying into it, reinforce what you need to do instead. Every time you hear the 'what if,' respond either with a positive statement or challenge it. You can challenge that voice rather than buying into those doubts. Answer with a very conscious, logical, knowing response.

"And I should make this a daily part of my routine as well? This shouldn't be just a specialized thing?"

That's right. Bob is going to be with you for a while.

"You know, with those internal distractions going on, I sometimes forget to focus on creating the sound, which seems to be the way that works best for most excellent players I know. I don't do enough work creating sound; I react to what comes out of my bell as opposed to creating it and imagining it as a finished product before I even physically start. I need to do a lot of that, and I know that, and yet I don't do that. What does that say?"

This is a common problem, but definitely something you can overcome. You just need to set up a schedule to practice that. Just like setting up a schedule to practice physically the pieces for Houston, I'd also encourage you to set up some mental practice time to focus on what we're going to cover.

"I seem to need some help with that."

When would you like to start?

Both Veronica and Brian were ready to begin. Having gone through their profiles individually, it was obvious that both were enthusiastic, talented musicians. At the same time, contrasting issues and styles meant that we would be focusing on different things. Everyone is unique, but as you will see, the skills and techniques I use in my program can be made specific to each and every individual, including both Veronica and Brian. It was now time to begin the real work.

If you're interested, you can go to www.Dongreene.com on the Internet. After you log in, you'll be able to complete the Artist's Survey and receive your own individualized printout, with a full analysis of your profile and specific recommendations on where you can make the most improvement.

CHAPTER TWO

Process Cues

BREATHE

The focus of the material in this chapter deals with familiarizing Veronica and Brian with their energy levels—in and out of auditions. I also introduced a critical concept to both of them: the process cue. This is a word or phrase that represents what you do when you're performing your best or what you think about in order to do well. You will see how both Veronica and Brian develop their process cues according to their own specific needs.

My second meeting with Veronica was the next afternoon, when she came out of her rehearsal. We went into the vestibule and found some comfortable chairs. After the other singers had gone, we went back to the previous day's conversation. She started out by mentioning the voices in her head. I told her I'd like to start knowing more about what the voices told her to do in order to sing well.

Think of two or three positive words that would help before you go on. What words capture your best singing, or what you need to do? Imagine that you're about to go on stage and you're hearing one of your teachers reminding you how to sing well. What would they say?

Veronica thought about this for a second. "I don't know," she replied, a little confused.

How about words like 'posture' or 'breathe' or 'flow'?

"I think it would be something more . . . not something physical. Something like, 'There's nothing to worry about, as long as you're thinking about the character and what the character has to do. Then there's nothing to be nervous about.' Something like that."

What about your good singing. What do you need to do to sing well? Or what do you do when you are singing well?

"I'm not sure."

I was trying to get Veronica to come up with a word that would capture her process when she was doing it correctly. I asked her to tell me about one of the best performances in her career.

"I did a recital last year, my graduation recital from the conservatory."

Why were you so good that day?

"I felt like everybody in the audience was really excited to listen to me."

What else?

She paused. "I was pretty well prepared. . . . "

What did you do with your voice? How did you sound?

"Pretty good. . . . I was a little nervous, but not terribly. I listen to the tape now and I know I could have sounded better."

What would you do to sound better?

"Breathe better."

Define 'better.' [I wanted her to be specific here.]

"It helps my voice . . . it helps support the tone."

How do you learn to breathe better?

"I don't know . . . by working at it."

[Before Veronica got stuck in her standard mode of thinking, I wanted her to look deeper at what was causing her nervousness.] We'll come back to your breathing. Let's talk about your fear of failure.

"OK," she said.

Let's assume that you're about to step out on stage and you're thinking about what could go wrong. What comes to mind?

She thought about this. "Things like, 'What if I crack on a high note?' . . . 'What if I forget the words?' . . . 'What if I don't express the aria very well?' . . . things like that."

Alright. There are two ways to deal with these. Do you work with any younger singers?

"A little bit with high school girls."

Let's say that you've been working with one of them for several months and then it's time for her to do a high school performance. Ten minutes before she goes out, she says, 'What if I crack on the high note?' What would you tell her?

"Oh God. . . . Oh God! You can't tell her that she won't . . . ," she hedged.

What could you tell her to do to prevent that from happening?

"I don't know. This is really hard."

When this happens to you before you go out, and you accept the 'what if's' as real possibilities, it can drive your activation level of 80 up to a 90. And if, at that point, you don't have a strategy to bring it down from the 90, it will stay there for quite a while, especially by thinking about it without any solution. So wouldn't you rather talk about it now? [This was a critical point in Veronica's thought process.]

"Oh, yeah." She laughs. "I'm just shocked that I can't come up with any examples."

Let me use a sports example. Have you ever watched any platform diving?

"Like in the Olympics? Yeah."

On back takeoffs, divers stand with only the balls of their feet on the platform. From that position, they can do back dives or inward somersaults. When they're doing inward two-and-a-half's, they spin in toward the platform. One of their fears is hitting their head. Now if they're standing there and thinking, 'I hope I don't hit my head,' it's very tough for them to go.

"I bet."

Coaches certainly don't want them to get too close, but they don't want them to be too far away either. If they push back too far, it's difficult for them to make the rotations. Then they don't spin enough and don't hit the water correctly. That can be painful. So the coaches want them jumping it in the right place. They use positive cue words or phrases. Rather than having them think about hitting their heads, they tell them, 'Jump to the right place.' If they do that, they'll be safer and start the dive well. So instead of thinking, 'Don't hit your head,' they say, 'Jump right,' as a positive cue.

"I see," Veronica said, nodding.

If they start thinking, 'What if I hit my head?' and 'That would really hurt,' it can lead to them thinking about being in the hospital. That would probably drive their activation level to a ninety. Then they get physically tight, and that makes it even tougher to do the dive. So they've learned to substitute positive process cues for each one of the 'what if's.' For 'What if I hit my head on the platform?' they substitute, 'Jump in the right place.'

"So how does this work in terms of singing?"

Positive process cues would be more helpful for you to think about than cracking on the high note. So what do you need to do to sing well?

"Well, I need to breathe, I need to relax . . . and I need to get into my part."

That reduces the anxiety.

"Yeah. But what if I tell myself that and then I don't do it?" She sounded skeptical.

That's just another 'what if.'

"Oh, no!"

When tough situations come up, when the stakes are higher and there's more pressure, the 'what if' gets louder and faster and you hear it more often. You can take it too seriously and start to buy into it: 'Well, what if it does happen? What if my voice cracks?' Once you buy into it, your activation levels rise dramatically.

"I see what you mean."

But you can challenge that and start dealing with it. Imagine yourself thinking, 'What if I forget the words?' Now, rather than buying into it, I would like you to challenge it and prove why it's not going to happen.

"I'm not going to forget the words," Veronica repeated to herself. "And so what if I do?"

How about, 'I've memorized the words. I've spent the time. I've gone through a thousand rehearsals. I know it in my sleep.' How's that? Or you could use your good sense of humor.

"I think that happened to me before that recital, actually. I was just out there saying to myself, 'There's a whole group of people here to hear me sing. This is crazy!' And I just started laughing because I didn't believe that you could do something like that. You just had to laugh." She smiled with the memory.

And your nervous activation of 85 went to a 70 or 75.

"Yeah. It's so exciting to believe that that can happen."

You did it! Your humor is a definite ally. When your humor kicks in, it's wonderful. But when you're too serious, when the 'what if's' are really dominating your thoughts, you're not laughing and your nervousness goes up.

"Yeah, it's stupid. Then you make yourself do things wrong. You're home and you sing through the arias before an audition and everything's fine, and then you get to the audition and you think, 'I can't do it. I can't do it right.' You make yourself screw it up."

Or you can allow yourself to sing well.

"Right, right. It's not that bad."

A key part in Veronica's ultimate success would be focusing on keeping those inner thoughts positive, as it is so often a critical element in stressful situations. She needed to challenge her "what ifs," use her sense of humor, and keep repeating her process cues. With those things in mind, she and I arranged to speak again the next day.

A TRAINING DIARY

My first phone call with Brian was the week after I got back from Syracuse. He was anxious to continue. I started by asking him if he had any afterthoughts from our session in Syracuse. He recalled that we had "hit a number of things." He remembered talking about his fear of failure and its relationship to internal distractibility. We had also discussed Bob.

Brian's face lit up. "Actually, I used him on Saturday night. He's the 'what if' guy, you know. 'What if you miss this note coming up?' 'What if you lose the count?' I just told him to back off," he said, triumphantly.

And how did that feel when you said that?

"That felt pretty good. I felt a little more in control."

Super. Did that add any humor to it?

"Actually, I took it as kind of 'professional.' You know it's like, 'Look Bob, I've got to do my job. I'm supposed to get all the right notes, so let's talk about this at a later time.' This was the first time I've tried that exact strategy out."

Good! [It sounded like Brian was making progress. It was time to narrow down specific auditions to work toward.] Now let's talk about the specific dates.

"Today, I got my packet from Houston. The dates are the 20th, 21st, and 22nd of May. I've already made my reservations."

That gives us a little less than six weeks.

"I'm going to request a mid-morning time on Monday the 22nd. That's the last day and the finals are later that day. So I'm hoping that I will come in . . . they will be tired, but I know they're a good section and they'll still be listening. So if I can go in there and prime myself, just walk in there and say, 'Boom, there it is,' they'll take me, no matter how many they have in the finals."

That's the right attitude.

"I want to go in and knock their socks off. No matter how many finalists, they'll add one more if I show them that I've got something."

Have they told you what pieces to prepare?

"Houston has about 25 or 26 excerpts. But they can throw anything at you and they all have to be perfect. No problem."

What do you like to do to prepare for it?

"In the next week, I would like to get my practicing planned out as far as doing specific things, not just going over the excerpts a number of times. I have thought of taking maybe the top five excerpts that I don't play as well as I would like to, working on at least one of them a day, and really working them over as far as playing them through the tuner, playing for the tape, playing them slower or faster, playing them in a different key, all sorts of ways you can do it. But there are a couple of excerpts, like the opening of *Rheingold*, that I just don't have."

Could you put the excerpts into three piles? One that you could nail in your sleep, one that you can do half-awake, and the third one we'll call challenging. And after you've done that, randomly pick one or two pieces from the first pile and play them, and then move to the second, and then play a few of the picks out of the third.

"Practice two out of column one, two out of column two. Two from each column? At a single practice session?"

Exactly.

"Should I work them over or just play them once or twice through?"

Right now, whatever seems appropriate, but separate this practice from your regular playing. And start building a routine into your practice and playing.

"But I play just excerpts and nothing else."

If you're doing scales or practicing other pieces before that, please take a break and go out of the room. Or even better, go outside before you start this audition prep routine.

"So make this a complete break? Because otherwise, I can start right in. Sometimes I'll do that with excerpts, as if it's the first excerpt of an audition. No warm-up even, sometimes. I'll just walk in and see what I can do."

Separate it so that you're doing it for a specific purpose.

"Any particular length to this session?"

What would be your longest time on stage for an audition?

"In an audition, probably the longest would be ten to twelve minutes."

Then go for twenty-five minutes, so you can play longer than you'd ever need to. You could build up to it over several days, certainly by the time we talk next time. In the meantime, just go in and play under the same conditions as you'd expect in Houston. If you're going to be standing in front of the music stand or sitting down, then do that and whatever else will help to approximate the circumstances. Come in with your horn, go through the excerpts and play your best.

"Now is that the session to do two of each from the three piles? That's this kind of practice?"

Yes. And before you go in, check your energy levels and see where you are. Are you going to be playing behind a curtain?

"Yeah, there's always a screen."

Okay, imagine that the people on the other side of the screen are there . . .

"So imagine a screen. . . ."

. . . and imagine those people and doing it for real. If you feel any extra energy, amplify it, bring it up. Put some pressure on yourself to play incredibly well. I want you to mimic the sense of playing in a real pressure environment.

"Okay."

But first try to quiet your mind. Deal with Bob or whatever you need to do to get there. And start using a routine so you can find one that works.

"Does this include checking energy levels?"

Yes, a scan of your body to check your activation level and also make sure that your muscles are relatively relaxed.

"But I put the pressure on myself. That's kind of opposite, isn't it? Because I'm trying to relax myself."

That's a good observation. Put the pressure on and then alleviate it.

"All in the same preaudition routine?"

Yes. You'll get used to it.

"So put the pressure on myself, imagine the screen, imagine everything else and then quiet my mind and relax my body. And this is after I've put pressure on myself?"

Yes.

"So what I'm doing is getting myself keyed up and then bringing myself down and then stepping into the practice room. . . ."

. . . and playing to the best of your ability. This is not a regular practice with warm-ups and technical exercises. This is Show Time.

"So that's when I actually walk in and play two from each level."

Yes.

"And I play them in that order? The ones that I can nail in my sleep and then the ones that are marginal and then the ones that are difficult."

Say, 'the ones that are challenging!'

"Yeah, I know that's important."

Eventually, you're going to give every excerpt a word. But we're not quite there yet. By next week, will you be able to play all of them?

"Oh sure. I mean I could do this, perhaps even twice a day."

Just go in there after your routine, go through the excerpts, play your best and finish. Go back to whatever else you were doing, and if you want to go through it again later, start with your routine again.

"Should I tape it? Because taping makes me nervous, even sitting at home."

Yes. That's important in creating the sense that you're performing.

"Okay, I'll tape it and then listen to it afterwards."

And write some notes.

"Okay, critical listening."

Not critical so much as what you need to improve, how you can do it better next time.

"So put it in positive terms; 'tone could be smoother' or 'slur could be more in tune.' Something like that?"

There you go!

"Not, 'that sucked' ... 'this was terrible' ... 'where'd you get that shaky sound?' Sometimes I listen and say to myself, 'Oh, you've got to be kidding!'" Brian laughed.

The last thing, Brian, is when you're playing these, if you make a mistake, do whatever you'd do if you were to make a mistake in the audition.

"Got it. Just go on."

Just go on. You're going to make a mistake in practice and then you can figure out how to keep on going and build that into your practice. So once you walk into the room to start, you're on. Do your best.

"Yeah, matter of fact, I might go as far as to let the tape go before I get into the room so I don't have the official thing of starting the tape by hitting the pause button. It will make it as close to the real thing as possible."

That's great.

"What else?"

The other thing is to keep notes when you're listening afterwards. Not just on the sound, but on what you've been working on and your progress, and what you've been experiencing and learning.

"So you want me to keep a training diary?"

Yeah. Keeping a diary allows you to keep a record of the positive steps you're taking. It will help you track your progress.

"I like that idea. You know, I did that once in a while as a student. I certainly haven't done it lately, but I know it helps."

You can start anytime you'd like.

"Give me a specific day."

Two weeks from today.

"Great. Now I've got a deadline. I work better when I've got some time limits. I've got the whole week off and sometimes I'll fritter it away. So that's probably enough for me for now. I'll call you in two weeks."

Veronica and Brian now had their first assignments. Veronica needed to use positive reinforcement, challenge her 'what ifs' and keep her precious sense of humor. Brian was going to start a training diary and build a routine into his daily practice schedule. He would arrange his excerpts into different categories and start putting pressure on himself to perform them well in mock sessions. Although they had two distinctly different strategies, the primary goal was to put both musicians back in control of themselves and their music.

CHAPTER THREE

Centering

NINETY MILES PER HOUR

Veronica and I spoke again a few weeks later, soon after she got home from Lake George. I was curious to see how her work with energy levels and her self-talk were going. What had happened in her performances—the effectiveness of her strategy and her ability to incorporate it into her singing—was going to be the template from which we moved forward.

"Hi, Don. How are you?"

Just fine, Veronica. It's good to be home. How did it go in Lake George?

"Pretty good. Things went well, but it was really hectic the last week. A lot of rehearsing, and then we had the double billing after the second opera opened up. It was pretty good, though. It was a good experience up there; it's a nice place to work."

Did *Gianni Schicchi* go well?

"Well, the first performance didn't go that great, but the second performance did. So at least we left on a good note," she laughed. "It was pretty stressful."

Were there only two performances?

"Yes. The two shows. But it ended up great so I look back at it with good feelings mostly. Compared to other places I've worked. So I've just been home and working on some of the stuff we talked about. It really did help me through *Gianni Schicchi* and the remaining performances of *Rigoletto* a lot."

Can you be more specific?

"Well, before any performance, I was very concerned about what the audience would think of me. I wanted to make sure I would do stuff they would like. It was kind of going on subconsciously, but I thought, 'That's not going to help me perform the way I need to if I'm worried about what they're thinking.' So at least I really, really tried to see that that was what I was feeling, and to try and just push that away. I think it did help, that I could give myself permission not to have to worry about what they were thinking. And it worked up there in Lake George."

Great!

"Where it didn't work though, was in a couple of auditions that I did this week. Because I thought, 'Hey, great! I'm good now! No problems. I'll be able to deal with it and not get nervous and not lose focus.' But in an audition yesterday, I sensed that when I was singing, the people listening to me weren't interested. And that made me lose my focus on what I was doing. It made me think that what I was doing was uninteresting. In the second piece I sang, they were interested, so it made me more interested in what I was doing and I felt better about what I did when I knew that they liked what I did.

But I wasn't happy that I had to have their approval of what I was doing in order to perform well."

What was this an audition for?

"It was for a management/agent type of thing."

When you say that you sensed that they either liked it or they didn't, what do you mean? [I wanted to get a better idea of what actually distracted Veronica.]

"Oh, just in their interest. I could see that they were looking around. I don't know exactly. They just didn't seem interested. Looking around, doing other things, possibly thinking about something other than me singing."

I've got you. And the second song was better?

"Yes. I could see that they were paying attention and smiling and thinking 'Oh, yeah! We like this.'" I found out afterwards that they didn't think I should be singing the first piece. They did think that I should be singing the second piece. But I don't feel that way; I feel like I should be singing both pieces. One is slow and romantic, and the other is light and playful. They make a good combination."

Are these pieces you chose or ones that they chose?

"I chose."

But you felt fine with both pieces before you went in? It was obvious that the pieces themselves weren't the cause of the problem.

"Yeah. I felt fine, perfectly fine. But I know that their interest in what I was doing affected my performance. I was upset that I lost my focus so easily."

Well, focus is an issue that we haven't talked about yet. Do you have other auditions coming up?

"Yes. A big one coming up on Labor Day weekend. I'm going to Chicago."

And what's that one for?

"For the Lyric Opera of Chicago. They have a program for young artists. They auditioned a bunch of people in May and June. Then they have a final round where they fly in twenty people and have them sing for the artistic director of the company."

Veronica had a chance here to win the final round of an important audition. This was a critical point to bring everything together, including improving her focus.

When do you want to start preparing?

"Oh, as soon as possible." We both laughed.

Let's go back to our discussions. We talked about process cues like 'relax' and 'breathe,' and that these are better than the 'what if's.'

"I keep on thinking about how you said that my activation runs at an 80, and that's what I felt yesterday. I am just too hyper right now. I have to calm down. What we talked about worked for me in Lake George. I was able to calm down. This audition yesterday, I didn't know how to calm myself down. I tried everything. I didn't know what to do."

When you talked about the first and second performances of *Gianni Schicchi*, you said the first one wasn't so good. Why?

"I had a hard time in the first performance really just focusing on what I had to do. I kept thinking of what was going wrong with other people in the cast and I also kept thinking, 'Oh, the audience isn't enjoying this,' or 'I didn't sing that as well as I should have.' I just couldn't do the job that I had to do."

So you were worrying about other singers and also about the audience?

"Yeah. Just feeling like I wasn't making any kind of impression."

And what made the second one different?

"With the second one, I felt the audience was enjoying it and people around me seemed to be a little more excited about doing it. I just focused on what I had to do."

This related directly to your ability to focus internally on the performance, as opposed to what's going on around you. Do you understand what a preperformance routine is?

"No."

And we didn't talk about Centering either, did we?

"No." She shook her head.

So when is your Chicago audition?

"It's a week from Saturday."

How many pieces do you have to prepare?

"Four in total. One's an aria from *Carmen* (and one's a Bernstein). And then there are two Rossini's."

Okay. How can you differentiate between the two Rossini's?

"One is much more lighthearted and one's more serious."

Can you rank them in terms of how confident you are when singing them? Say the aria you're the most confident about is a one, the next one is a two, the next is a three, and the one you're least confident in singing is a four. Can you do that?

"Sure." She thought about it for a second. "The serious Rossini would be a one, the lighthearted Rossini would be a two, the *Carmen* a three, and the Bernstein a four."

And you have all four of them memorized, and you're singing them all?

"Yes."

Good. When I talk about a pre-performance routine, I'm talking about what you do in the last ten or fifteen minutes before you go on, whether it's on stage for a dress rehearsal, a recital or an audition. The last ten or fifteen minutes.

"Okay."

For each of those pieces, I want you to come up with cue words that are meaningful for you, words that help you to sing them well. Or about how you sing when you're singing your best. Take the more serious Rossini. Give me two or three words that capture either why you sing it well, what you need to do to sing it well, or how you sing it when you're singing it well.

"Oh, I see. So how . . . ?"

It goes back to the cue words, which for you were 'breathe' or 'relax.' But these need to be more specific for each individual piece.

"Okay. So two or three words about what it's like when I sing it well."

Or what you need to do to sing it well. Try not to get too technical. It is important that process cues be separate from technical music jargon.

"A process cue for each aria?"

Yes. But now for the toughest one.

"Uh oh!" she exclaimed, laughing.

First, I need to teach you a process to bring your energy down. Have you done any type of meditation or relaxation training?

"Uh, not really."

Okay. You're about to learn.

"Oh, God." She laughed again

It won't hurt! The good news is that you already know how to breathe from your lower abdomen. Because this technique, known as Centering, is based upon proper breathing technique.

"Okay."

For the next couple of days, I want you to lay on the floor and put one hand on your stomach and one hand on your chest, unless you can just do this automatically. Do this deep abdominal breathing for three, four, or up to ten times a day, with your stomach rising without your upper chest moving. The first sequence of breaths is proper abdominal breathing for up to ten breaths. Breathe in through your nose and out slowly through your mouth. That's step one. [Veronica jotted this down.] Number two is going to sound a little bit weird to you, unless you've taken Zen.

"No, I haven't." We both laughed.

Okay. You're going to have fun with this one. It's going to be a little bit of a challenge. Have you ever heard of Chi, the life force, or Ki?

"I've heard of it."

Well, it originates from your center. Your center is defined as two inches below your navel and two inches into your body.

"Okay."

So lay on the ground and put your hand two inches below your navel and push in a little bit so that you can define that point. And then while you're taking those ten breaths, bring your focus to your hand and be at your center. Get out of your head and into your center. If it helps you to close your eyes, then close them. Leave the external surroundings, get out of your head and get inside.

"That's probably a bit difficult."

This is your challenge. Don't get critical about your performance. There are no right or wrongs. You're not supposed to nail it the first time.

"Okay. I understand."

So have some fun with it, and we'll see. Does that sound all right?

"Sounds good!"

This will be a big part of your preperformance routine. It'll help you relax more and get more focused after you learn how to do it. So we've got to go through a learning sequence and what we're doing right now is just doing parts. These will be parts that we're going to build on. In the meantime, play around with it. Does that make sense?

"Yeah."

Do this several times a day.

"Do it every hour?"

You can if you want. [We both laughed.]

And also come up with process cues for each of the four pieces.

"Okay. Can I call you on Friday?"

That's good. Please get a pad or a little notebook and keep some notes on this stuff, and if something comes up, you'll remember it when we talk next time.

"Yeah. Great! So I'll talk to you on Friday."

SEAMLESS

Brian and I got together again two weeks later, and I was interested in finding out how his practice sessions were going.

He quickly brought me up to date on his progress, starting with his training diary.

"Well, I started my training diary. It was kind of sporadic. Saturday I hardly did anything. My gig on Sunday was interesting because I had written down that I was playing first and it was relatively early in the morning. I had to play out more than usual, giving downbeats and stuff, and I'm not always comfortable doing that. I practice that kind of thing but don't enjoy it too much. I wrote down some good things and some bad things that pretty much mirrored my physical and mental state. Some stuff was great and some stuff wasn't, but I managed to maintain control, which I considered a victory. It's not so much being nervous as it is that I use too much tension. I think I've been able to differentiate between the two."

Good. What does the tension feel like?

"When I take my air, I start shaking. And then I start worrying about it and it gets worse. So what I did in the Gabrielli, I was shaky during the whole Gabrielli. . . . I don't know what set me off, but I just kept going. I didn't miss any notes because of it and I didn't let it get any worse. But I didn't have the skills to get it any better, so the whole piece pretty much remained like that."

So you take in air and that makes you feel shaky?

"I probably don't take in enough air and that's part of it. It's kind of a vicious circle. If you don't take enough air and you use too much tension to play, your muscles start rebelling, I suppose."

And where do you feel that? Which muscles?

"Well, where I feel it is in my lips. Like, if I take a breath and I'm ready to play, it feels like the embouchure isn't steady."

And what do your chest and shoulders feel like?

"You know, my arms will feel a little shaky also, from the tops of the shoulders down the arms, and when you feel like that, you stop breathing because you start focusing on your shakiness rather than what you ought to. What I tried to do was continue to focus on my breathing. I couldn't get it any better, but I prevented it from getting any worse."

While that's going on, what are your thoughts?

"Well, it kind of surprised me. My thoughts maybe a year ago would have been, 'Oh, great! Here it goes again!' But I made a concerted effort to just say, 'Okay. Here's what's going on. You know what to do.' I hadn't practiced enough to calm down and take better breaths. I did it to some extent, but not enough apparently to combat it effectively and bring myself back to normal. But I did prevent myself from getting any worse, so it was really not that bad. I noticed it, but I don't even know if anybody else noticed it. And I didn't miss any notes as a result of it, which was definitely an improvement."

Good. What else did you follow up on?

"I had a couple of things that I want to discuss with you. I wrote some notes. Although yesterday and so far today, I've made improvements, in general, I need ways to incorporate more mental work and visualizing into my practice routine. Even though I discussed that with you before, I know that I don't need to go see a teacher. I know everything I need to know. I've studied with the best and I've got notes and lesson tapes from the best teachers in the business and they taught me well, but for some reason, I don't seem to do these things. I don't follow the notes and I don't do enough mental work. I'm definitely physically oriented, and I've had a number of the teachers tell me that. That's not all bad, but yesterday I really made a concerted effort to incorporate more mental training into my practice."

Does it feel good when you do that?

"Yeah, it does. For example, for Monday I wrote down thirty minutes of notes in my training diary, then I did an hour of audition practice with some relaxation thrown in. I did fifteen minutes of just experimenting. I was watching TV— practicing with the television on is good once in a while—and I played part of a lick that I've been having difficulty with. I just tried to run it through different variations while not focusing on it. Then I did twenty minutes of listening to the only time that I did the audition prep training, the one that we talked about two weeks ago. I listened to that. I did it on Thursday and finally listened to it yesterday. And then I did forty-five minutes of solid practicing."

And how did all that feel?

"Some good things and some bad things. I was mostly picking different sections of each piece apart. I focused on a couple of licks and did them in different ways. I had the metronome going and taped things a couple of times. I would have to consider yesterday a very good day. But lately, I've had a lack of motivation. Part of it's because I had viral pleurisy in my right lung and that knocked my whole vacation off. I wrote down, 'I know what to do. Why am I not doing it?' in my training diary."

What's the answer to that?

"I'm not motivated. I know what to do but I'm not doing it because I'm not motivated. I also put down a lack of focus and organization in practice. I need ways to add structure. I was going to look to you to help me. Maybe if I organized my training diary a certain way and got a practice routine going, the two would help each other."

You might want to commit to following a routine with your practice.

"Which I do not have. My practicing has been sporadically

brilliant, like getting ready for an audition. But in general, I have really fallen off the habit of organized routines."

Are you ready to start now?

"Yes. Actually, I kind of started it yesterday, but I want to keep it going. So give me some parameters."

I shook my head. Well, I can't. You're the only one who knows them. When you decide what it is, commit to it, write it down, and follow it. A regular length of time and a general structure of what you want to do within it. It's important that you structure your routine according to your own personal needs. I can't do that for you.

"Okay. One thing I did that was positive was that I took my clock off the living room wall. And what I do is set the alarm and say, 'Okay, I'm going to do such and such minutes,' and then I don't look at the clock or my watch until the alarm goes off. I find that that's effective."

That's good. Now that you've arranged a time frame, you need to implement your goals. The other thing, Brian, are your goals really clear?

"No. I mean the long-term goal is going to the audition and getting the excerpts, but that seems somewhat vague in a way, because I don't seem to be able to practice effectively toward the long-range goal."

You need to make them more immediate and real. Even from now until next week.

"I see. In the one audition training session that I did, I divided everything up into the ones, twos and threes. I had one as 'Very Confident,' two as 'In Progress,' and three as 'Challenging.' These could be more immediate goals. The second category would be the most lengthy, but I put a good number in the first. There are still a few problems with a couple of those. If I'm very confident about them but I can't play them in my sleep ... ?"

Then they go in with the twos.

"It's funny, I wound up having another category between one and two. Maybe I could use that as the repository for the ones that I'm very confident about but that still have a glitch or two. So that could be one-a. Those are close but not quite. And then the twos would be ones that I definitely can't play the first time and feel confident, and the threes are the ones I'm having difficulty with."

Challenging, not difficult, remember?

"Yeah, challenging. Well, I think that I say that because I figure I should be able to play all of them."

Do you know anything about Centering?

"I know something about it. Basically just try to clear your mind of all other extraneous thoughts. Let them flit about, but don't give them any real power and just focus on what you really need to focus on, which for me would be what I want to come out of the horn. Instead of worrying about shaking or not getting a good breath, I should think about the next note I want to play and focus on that as much as I can."

That is a good description of how it works. But let me describe a step-by-step process that you can start to practice and use.

"So this is a step-by-step routine?"

Yes. But it takes a minimum amount of time. Basically, you're going to take three deep breaths and simultaneously engage in three different mental processes. With the first breath, on the inhale, you think about a full and deep breath.

"Okay. I'm going to write this down." Brian grabbed a pen and paper.

On the inhale, breathe slowly in through your nose, and pay attention only to your breath.

"Okay, so on the first breath, inhale fully, focus only on. . . ."

Getting a good breath.

"Good intake. Okay."

On the exhale, let out all the muscle tension. Drop the energy and make your arms, shoulders or neck feel very heavy or loose.

"Okay, focus on relaxation. . . ."

Letting all the tension out with the breath going out. On the next breath, be at your center. And this gets a little bit esoteric, but it simply means your center of mass or center of gravity. It's two inches below your navel and two inches into your body, toward your backbone.

"I'll try and visualize that."

Or actually while you practice, put your hand there and try and bring your mind down there. Get out of your head and into your center.

"I've heard this. The Yoga books I've read mention it, that's it's supposed to be the center. Because when the Yogis were breathing it seems that everything is focused there. Okay, so on the second breath inhale and exhale?"

Yes, but focus on being at your center. On your third breath, on the intake, say a positive word or phrase, a process cue that captures your best playing. Something a teacher would say to you that's really positive about performing your best, but not necessarily something technical.

"The one I'm using right now is 'relaxed and confident.' How's that?"

That's okay, but the relaxed part is going to come with the first breath. Let me give you an example and then ask you to find a better one. Maybe something like 'flowing' or 'smooth' or 'pure'? I don't know.

"So it would be one or two words that are positive. One that did work for me was 'seamless.'"

There you go.

"This was for a specific problem I was having. I was putting a gap between notes in a particular passage, so I just focused on 'seamless' and did the same thing. It came out right. And there are others I can use."

Find one for the next week and use it.

"Exclusively?"

What I don't want you to do is be sitting there searching for it when you're in the process. Come up with one and try it out several times, and either use it or find a better one and use that one.

"Okay. And the positive statement should be about what?"

About how you play your best or whatever word captures what you need do to play your best.

"Okay. And this is on the intake of the third breath?"

Yes. And while you're doing these first two-and-a-half breaths, try to look at a nondescript spot on the floor and defocus your eyes or just close them.

"Closed eyes works better for me, at least now."

Then, on the exhale of this third breath, open your eyes and turn your focus or energy out. Direct your full attention to a specific point on the stage as you focus your energy out, like, 'Here it comes!' You're not going to actually say it, but think it to yourself.

"Like extending Ki or Chi?"

Exactly!

"All right. So this is something I could do anytime?"

Practice it several times in the next few days. Whenever you feel a lot of nervousness come on, let this be your response. When you're doing your audition prep excerpts, you can use it right before you go in. After a few days, you'll get comfortable with it. Then put some extra pressure on yourself and use it to play well.

"I practice for a few days in neutral and then crank it up? So I'll be starting that kind of practice before I talk to you next time?"

Right. Imagine yourself playing in a tough situation or an audition or take out one of your pieces and have this be your response to it.

"Or I could try and get the physical manifestation going by running in place and then seeing if I can get my heart beat down and get relaxed, because that's often what it feels like."

Now we're talking. That's it. Try to induce the physical reaction, then use the Centering to deal with it.

"Okay. I will practice that. It will be a good way to start before every practice session or rehearsal. I've got a rehearsal tomorrow morning, so I'll go over this a few times. I'm playing first horn unassisted on the *Britten War Requiem* and of course I want to do well. That will be a pressure situation."

So play with it today and find a way that will start to work for you.

"So what you want me to do is practice this and commit to doing my diary and my routine. I made a good start on that yesterday and today."

Good, keep it going.

"I'll let you know about all this and hopefully I'll be prepared to read you my practice routine next time we speak."

Super!

"This is the kind of motivation I needed, a little push. Thanks."

You're welcome, Brian. Have a good week.

As you can see, the process of Centering is so essential that it should be incorporated into every performer's daily routine. Both Veronica and Brian needed more control over their performance energy, and the ability to Center would allow them to play around with various levels and thereby learn how it feels to go from a higher energy level to a lower, more controllable one. This powerful technique eventually becomes second nature during important performances. When its done correctly, it can have a profound effect on one's energy, focus, and competence under pressure.

Centering comes from the Japanese martial art of Aikido and from Western psychology. It was developed in the seventies by Dr. Robert Nideffer, an Olympic sports psychologist who had studied Aikido in Japan and earned his black belt. He was my mentor. His technique has proven effective with competitive athletes and it continues to be a chosen strategy with world-class musicians and even top business executives. After eighteen years' experience using it with elite performers, Centering remains the single most effective tool I've found for preparing elite performers to do their best under pressure.

CHAPTER FOUR

From Your Center

THE HUB OF THE WHEEL

Now that I had introduced both process cues and Centering
to Veronica and Brian, it was time to start integrating the
two skills into their specific performances. For Veronica, this
meant focusing her energy in her center and then singing from
this energy source with the help of her process cue. But first,
I wanted to see how she was doing familiarizing herself with
the entire Centering process. This was three days after our
last call.

I want to go back to my notes of our last conversation. Let's
start with the breathing. Tell me about how it went.

"Well, it was pretty good. I liked doing it. With about half
of them, I wasn't thinking of other things. But I can't say that
I ever completely left the external surroundings."

This isn't supposed to be an out of body experience.

"Oh . . . okay." She laughed.

But it is supposed to get you less distracted or less concerned with outside things and more focused on one point.

"I would say that I definitely did that four or five times, and then thoughts would creep in."

Was it arduous?

"No, no."

We're going to build on that then. I first needed to see whether that was unpleasant, uncomfortable, or impossible for you to do.

"No, it wasn't."

And it sounds like you could do it.

"Oh yeah!"

Then you just need to practice it a little bit more for the next few days. So that's good; that's step one. Did you feel, for those four or five times, that you actually got out of your head and down to your center?

"Uh. . . . yeah. . . . I think I got a little piece of that."

Well, since this is your first experience with it, you're off to a good start.

"Oh good."

Did you come up with the cue words for those four pieces?

"Yeah, I did. I hope I did it right. One word is the same in all of them. Is that okay?"

We'll see. Take me through them one at a time.

"For the serious Rossini piece, I wrote down that when I'm singing it best I feel 'calm' and 'connected,' and my voice is 'steady throughout.' I don't get overexcited at any one place. When I'm singing it, I feel like I'm alone and I become unaware of people listening."

We're going to need to get to that one, because that pertains not just to these pieces, but to your inside-out focus. That's fantastic!

"Oh good."

And the other Rossini piece?

"I think about 'words' or 'text' and also 'calm' or 'in control' and that same feeling of being alone."

Okay. What do you mean by "in control"?

"Well, the piece has a lot of fast singing in it, yet I never feel like it's a runaway train. I'm still singing every note, even though it's really fast."

Wonderful! So pick either 'words' or 'text.' Which one would it be?

"Oh . . . 'words.'"

So there are two good ones, 'words' and 'in control.' Super. Then the *Carmen*?

"Okay. I don't know if it makes sense, but when I'm singing it very powerfully or speak strong and really simply, I'm not doing anything too much, and I'm calm."

'Strong' and 'simple'?

"Yes. And the last one was Bernstein. And I'm 'absorbed' in it and 'connected.' That's all I could come up with. But I used 'connected' already."

That's not a problem. But as opposed to the other three pieces, this one doesn't sound like you're as far along and committed as the others. It still sounds like you're searching a little bit.

"Well, it's funny . . . because it's the easiest one to connect with emotionally, but it is hard to sing. But I never have a problem getting absorbed into it. I can get absorbed into it pretty easily and I don't get as distracted when I sing it."

There's the inside-out focus.

"But it is the hardest to sing."

Why?

"Vocally. It has some vocal things that are difficult."

Okay. Think about this for a second. Let's say you go to a great teacher or a voice coach that you really respect and say, 'I've got a question for you. This Bernstein piece is difficult. Can you help me with it?' After they listen to you sing it, what would they say for advice to help you get past the difficult part?

"Hmm. I guess when I go through the difficult part, they would probably say that I was acting like I was scared of it, so I was cutting off my voice and not singing as well as in the rest of the piece. So I would need to . . . ?"

You're right on track. I'm hearing 'scared' and 'cutting off your voice.' So what is the correction? What would they tell you to do instead of being scared?

"Well, it's like in the *Carmen* . . . because there was the one place where I came up with 'strong.' When I thought I had to be even more powerful, I was able to get through it."

Aaaahhhhh.

"So it's probably the same thing."

Okay. So could we say 'absorbed' and 'strong' or 'powerful'?

"Yeah! That's good!"

We're there. We'll come back to those later.

"Okay."

Let's go to the issue of your awareness of other performers, your concerns about the audience, and being distracted by outside things. They all go together. Do you buy that?

"Yes!"

Imagine yourself standing on stage. See yourself as the center of a hub, the middle of a wheel, standing in that center.

"Okay."

Now there are all sorts of things that can pull you out of that center, whether it's your being aware of somebody watching you, somebody making noise, someone opening a door and coming into the hall, or your being too concerned about the audience. These things will pull you out of your center and put you into an outside-in orientation. But you want to be singing from your center, from inside-out.

"Yeah."

It's like a bicycle wheel with spokes going out. Everything outside tends to pull you out of your center. Instead of seeing that image, see yourself now standing on the stage and being able to get centered and then singing from there. Do you see how that works?

"Yeah."

Hold that thought. Now from that place, you can project your voice out to where you want it to go, rather than be involuntarily pulled by outside things. So you can project your voice out, but you stay at your center.

"That's hard to do because you have to trust that your voice is actually going to get out there, without jumping up and down and screaming."

So you need to trust that your voice will get out there?

"Yes. Without doing extra things."

Such as . . . ?

"Like, I think I sometimes do things with my body. I'll stick my head out sometimes, or take a step or just have a general posture that's leaning forward. Just a further assurance that I'll get out there, but it never helps."

Singing from your center is very powerful and it's one of the most helpful things you can do in performances and auditions.

"Oh yeah, my audition. . . ."

Tell me again about the audition.

"It's in Chicago, I leave a week from today and the audition is a week from tomorrow. It's for the Lyric Opera of Chicago Young Artists' Program, and it's the final round."

So you've already been through some of the others? How did they go?

"Okay . . . uh . . . let's just say they were okay auditions. I guess they were obviously good enough to get to this round, but they weren't the best."

How many people are trying out?

"There are about twenty. I don't know how many positions there are. I assume they'll hire four to six people."

Well, I'll give you a few more things to do right now and then we're going to make sure that they work. When you're not singing well, what muscles or parts of your body are tight?

"When I'm not singing well, usually I have all kinds of neck and jaw tension, and I can't get my abdominal muscles to make any difference in my singing. I just can't, no matter how much I try."

Because they're too tight?

"Yeah. Because it doesn't matter how much air I can push up. It's just not connected. And if my jaw's too tight, it's not going to get through. It's like being very uncoordinated."

And when you're singing well, your neck, jaw and stomach are all . . . what?

"They're all working but they're much more flexible, and my posture's better."

When you were doing your breathing, did you feel that you could just as easily do it sitting up?

"I think I could."

Okay. Take the breathing from lying down to doing it sitting up, but certainly with good posture.

"Okay."

Then take nine good breaths. On the first three breaths, as you breathe in, pay attention to your abdominals and getting a good breath. It might help when you're doing this to close your eyes. On the exhale, consciously relax your neck and jaw for three breaths. So on your inhale for those breaths, you're working on your stomach. On the exhale, you're working on being flexible and relaxing your jaw and neck. I'm not talking about getting sloppy and loose and letting your head fall, but finding the right level and being relatively relaxed. So does that make sense?

"Yes."

For the next three breaths, be at your center. Think of it as your base. It's a very powerful place to sing from. That's where martial artists, like in Karate and Aikido, fight from.

"Oh, really?"

Yeah. They don't fight from their head. They fight from

their center. I want you to see it as a source of your power and energy. What you're doing is getting in touch with that.

"Okay."

Now, on the last sequence of three breaths, go back to your cue words. Start with the serious Rossini, and on the first two breaths, say your cue words to yourself.

"All right. In my head?"

Yes. So you're still paying attention to your abdominals and saying 'calm' and 'connected' for those two breaths.

"Right."

But say them with conviction. Don't just go through the motions. Really get in touch with what they feel like and mean. Make them powerful for you.

"Right."

On the inhale of the third breath, get in touch with your center. On the exhale, open your eyes and narrow your focus to a point somewhere in front of you. Then, from your center, project that energy out to that point. Are we okay so far?

"Uh huh."

Do this sequence until you have it memorized and it flows. Practice it five or ten times until you're comfortable with it. Then try it with the *Carmen* and the other Rossini piece, using their cue words.

"Okay."

After you get the mechanics down, sing the first few bars, projecting your energy from your center to that point through your voice.

"Ahh. Okay."

I don't know how many notes that is, maybe thirty seconds

from the beginning of each piece. Because right now, our focus is on getting each of these started correctly. And after you do that, you're on cruise control. The words will cue you to remember what you need to do to sing well.

"So once I get this sequence of breaths and everything down, I should start to sing right away?"

Yes, do that for the first piece and then leave the room. Get a drink of water or do something else before you start the centering sequence for the next one. Make each of them a separate event.

"Okay."

This isn't what you'll necessarily be doing before an audition, but we're going through a learning progression first. Ultimately, it will be less than nine breaths and the cue words may change. In fact, by the next time we talk, things may start changing.

"Great."

So that's it for now. I'd like you to practice this several times a day. And then next time we talk, we can make refinements based upon your experiences and your feedback. And then we can start to work on the Bernstein.

"Oh . . . great." She laughed.

But by then, this technique will be in place and it can help you with it.

"Oh good."

When would you like to talk again?

"How's Monday?"

Super.

"I have an audition that evening around eight forty-five."

Really?

"Yeah, but it's not an important one."

That's wonderful. Do you know what you're going to be singing?

"I haven't picked it yet. But I figured that I would choose one that was challenging."

If that's the case, can we talk Monday morning?

"Sure."

We can take the next step and then apply it Monday night at the audition. How many pieces?

"Just two, but I choose what I start with."

Please come up with cue words for those.

"Well, it will be the same ones that I already have."

Okay. Well, we're right on track.

The idea with Centering effectively in the beginning lies in one's ability to be in tune with one's body. By focusing on her breathing, her tense muscles, and her physical center, Veronica was in a good position to control and focus her energy. As you will see with Brian in the next section, he was experiencing similar progress through Centering, but in a different way from Veronica.

WARM AIR AND FLOAT

I spoke to Brian one week after our last session.

"Hi, Don. How are you?"

Fine. How's it going with you?

"Well, it's been a very interesting week. I did a lot of the Centering. I practiced it quite a bit. I used it and I had two very good Britten *War Requiem*'s. I got a lot of compliments and I played very well. So I practiced it and I got to use it under pressure. I still need to work more on being able to relax over the entire length of a concert, because I still wind up feeling tension and not having the tools, either physically or mentally, to stay relaxed. There's a gradual creeping in of tension even as I try to let it out."

Okay.

"And I got more opportunities to try it out because the principal's chops have really been in bad shape. He still has that rash, so I may well have to play the whole concert. We have four run-outs in a row and Shostakovich's *Fifth Symphony* has a very big horn part. I've been playing the big solos, the ones that I thought would get me scared. They probably will a little, but I'm prepared to play them and I told the principal that if he needs me, I'll be there. I'm looking at it as an opportunity."

It really is.

"More than likely, probably Wednesday, I'll be playing first on the Shostakovich, so I'll just keep working on these things."

Well, talk me through it.

"Okay. Sometimes I'd start out a session with the breathing exercise, sometimes in the middle. Often I'd do it at the end and a couple of times during the rehearsal, and then in the concert. The way my sinuses are right now, I usually breathe through my mouth for intake and exhale. I wound up breathing in probably faster than you would want. I wasn't just trying to get that wisp of air in. I was pretty much breathing as if I were taking an exaggerated breath for the horn, slower than I would normally and probably a little more fully, but still focusing on good intake. Then I would hold it for just a fraction and let it out, and focus on my shoulders and neck especially. And then on the second one, my inhale and exhale would be both visualizing the center point. I remember that when I really get into the groove and get centered, I get this ticklish feeling right about where you described the center would be, and get that kind of half-smile and sense of contentment."

That's great!

"I would visualize it and focus on it as much as I could. For the third breath, I wouldn't close my eyes, especially on stage or rehearsal. I would focus on the back of the hall, where I ought to project, and my positive statement was usually 'warm air,' or 'confidence,' or 'projection.'"

Okay.

"And then on the exhale, I would imagine my sound going out. So specifically for my purposes right now, I can't do any better than that."

Brian, that sounds really good!

"And it worked. I don't have enough tools, like I said. There are times in the Britten concert where we really have to sit there for a time while the chamber orchestra plays, and I could not get comfortable. I didn't fidget, but I could feel my back and shoulders getting a little more tense, and every once in a while I would try to stretch out a little. You know, you can't do too much on stage. If I'd had my druthers, I would have put my horn down and climbed out of my chair and stretched out, but you can't do that." He laughed. "That's what I would have done if I'd been home. But I was able to keep excess tension from creeping in and I did some very good playing."

Good for you.

"So that's definitely a step forward. That's how I look at it."

Boy, you've already refined it.

"Yeah. You probably didn't give me too many specifics on purpose."

You've just taught me some things. Well, that's a lot of good progress. Keep on using it and refining it and finding the best way for it to work for you.

"Okay, so keep practicing that everyday?"

Yes. And when you're on stage, use it. The ideal situation would be where you were flooded with extra pressure and then you used Centering as an ally.

"This week is going to be unbelievable if I have to sit in and play that Shostakovich because it's got a lot of things that I have difficulty with, or have had in the past. I've spent the last few days making a breakthrough. I've gone through some old notes from my teacher in Chicago. I've been doing something slightly wrong for many years and I just corrected it. It's taken pretty quickly, and all of a sudden I've got a lot more ability to play in the soft dynamics. I've made my articulations more of what I want. At my stage, that's a major breakthrough, actually. So I feel a little less anxiety about the Shostakovich because there are a lot of soft entrances that are solo. I'd hate to mess those up."

Can you see yourself playing this piece well?

"Actually I can, but I haven't been working on that specifically. What I've been doing is having the music in front of me and saying, 'Okay, here it is,' and then taking a breath, playing it and feeling comfortable with it and being confident that it's going to come out like I want. That's the kind of practicing I've done. I hadn't been actually sitting here saying, 'Okay, imagine you're on stage and it's the concert.' I haven't really been doing that."

Could you do that a few minutes a day?

"So visualize pressure situations and apply the Centering techniques?"

Yes. See yourself getting to a much better place, with a half-smile on your face, prepared to play it well, and then see yourself nailing it.

"So see a positive result. This is something I can do at home."

When's your first night with the Shostakovich?

"The first performance will be Thursday night."

And the first rehearsal?

"Wednesday morning. I play it Thursday, Friday, and Saturday on the road, and then Sunday we play it here for a contributor's concert."

I'd love to talk with you Thursday after rehearsal. You know, last time you mentioned something about your lips. I recall that you said that you feel tension there sometimes.

"Yeah. I've pretty much solved that. It's kind of technical. I had forgotten to set my embouchure on relaxed chops and then I was applying even more pressure and tensing. So I remembered to form a more relaxed embouchure that gives me more 'meat' around the mouthpiece. And with my full lips that's a distinct advantage. That's really helped."

Good.

"We had a rehearsal tonight at Hamilton College. It's one of the better halls in this entire region. It's a great place. So I stuck around afterwards and played a few things for a good friend and everything came out great. Just using this technique makes things a lot easier."

I'm glad.

"I certainly have a lot more confidence. I'm able to do more of what I want. I had a physical impediment and I've taken a pretty big step in eliminating it. All that stuff has just happened in the last three or four days."

The other note I had was that you talked about some problems that lead to a lack of motivation. I'm just not hearing that now.

"Yeah. That was the case back then. It's funny. . .when you find a new way of playing things or get rid of an old problem that's been dogging you for years, that tends to get your motivation going. And with the Shostakovich, that's certainly got me going. But I have to bring my level up a little or I'm not going to play this well. I still do have an old problem that when I see something loud, I use way too much tension. I use more energy than I ought to and I try and play too loud rather than just trusting that I'll project fine. I overdo it."

Maybe that comes back to our Centering third breath and perhaps finding a better cue. You said "projection" or "warm air."

"I'm not sure that covers it."

So maybe for the Shostakovich, use a different one for your final cue. And I certainly don't know what that is, but I'm sure you can find one so you don't overdo it.

"How about 'float'?"

Something like that.

"Yeah. I just thought of that. It should just 'float' out. I'm using way too much tension and it binds me up. I can't be as flexible as I need to be and my air is locked up. I can feel my stomach muscles, which you're not supposed to."

So does 'float' capture all that?

"Uh, no. But it's a good start. You 'float' the sound out because that's a sense of ease, as opposed to hammering the sound out, which is what I have a tendency to do. I could probably come up with a couple of good ones, but 'float' is a good start."

Brian, this is a great opportunity to adapt it to the situation and watch it work for you. And also to use the visualization ahead of time to set that up; to preset that in your mind.

"Okay. So before the rehearsal, I should visualize. And tomorrow's practice could set me up pretty nicely, I imagine."

Try to go through it before you even get there.

"Yeah, but tomorrow I have the day off until the concert tomorrow night. That's the one in Hamilton. But I have the whole day of practicing to prepare myself."

Go through it in your mind first, then go through it physically. Put yourself in a situation and then actually play it.

"Okay. And imagine myself there on stage and having to play the solo maybe twice and saying to myself, 'I'm going to play it even better this time.' How's that?"

There you go.

"That kind of positive approach, rather than saying, 'Oh, shit! I'm going to screw it up this time.' You know, I also used that Bob thing. The Britten had gone so well on Friday and there's one place where we come in cold, and I'm the lead voice on that. And out of nowhere, I heard Bob starting to rumble, saying, 'Oh boy, you got that yesterday, but what if you miss it today and splatter all over the place?' So I told him to just back off."

Alright! Good for you!

"Didn't miss it."

That's great, Brian.

"So he just kind of shut up. It's funny, he shifted. He was over on the left side this time instead of the right side."

He just wanted to keep your attention.

"So I told him, 'Look. It ain't gonna happen, Bob,' and it didn't. It was a little closer than I would have cared for though, because he was still hanging on. He almost tried to knock the mouthpiece off or something, but I didn't let him."

Well, he's not going to go away easily.

"No, I don't expect that. Bob's going to be there for a while. He'll pop up when I least expect it."

But that's okay, as long as you have a strategy.

"And it's worked the two times it's come up. It hasn't happened very often, which is really an improvement. I'm just focusing on playing as well as I can, rather than 'what if.' So I could do myself a world of good by doing some mental training tomorrow."

You could imagine yourself in a pressure situation or even do something physical to mimic how you'd be feeling, and then center before you actually play one of the pieces.

"Maybe do something like run in place and get myself all pumped up, or make myself really nervous."

And trust that the Centering will get you where you need to be to play well.

"Yeah, that will give me something to do tomorrow. My training diary has been off and on. I am at least keeping track of my practice every day. But some nights, the last thing I've wanted to do is come home and write stuff."

I'm sure.

"But I do remember things. I know that I'm telling you more than I've written in the training diary, but it's uppermost in my mind. I just looked through the notes because we talked about getting my practice routine better established. This is something I've wanted to do; I've got all these good notes and I'm not using them, so I've started going through them and I picked this up and thought, 'I remember that. I should try this.' And it was like . . . bing!"

Ah. Isn't it wild the way that works?

"Yeah. It finally took twelve years to sink in completely. It had sunk in to some extent, and I was close at times, but I'd always fall back on my old habits."

It's easy to do. But it sounds like you're doing much better. Let's figure out a time to talk again.

"Hey, now we're talking! I feel that this has been a big burden off me because I think I've finally figured out something that's been holding me back. I know that there has been some impediment and it isn't just mental. There's a physical component to it too."

There usually is.

"Yeah. It's just an old habit. This may not be the absolute cure for everything, but I honestly think that I'm not a 'mouthpiece of the week' person. I don't think that the horn is holding me back, although this new Berg horn certainly has been an improvement over the old Schmidt. But I always go back to me." He laughed. "Not the instrument, not everybody around me, but this had been holding me back and I think I've discovered a good chunk of it, if not most of it."

That's great.

"And I'll just continue to work on it and see what happens. You know, I've got to do it. I mean, the principal horn is counting on me. He'll be sitting right next to me playing assistant so we'll make it a team effort. He knows my weaknesses and he'll help me through it."

I have faith in you.

"Thanks. I think it's going to go just fine. But I won't leave anything to chance. I've been working over some of the entrances that I think are going to be a little scary. I've been trying to use more of my right brain. All I have to do is hear that high G and play it and it's coming out well just about every damn time."

Oh, that's great.

"Now I guess my task is to make sure that once I'm in the rehearsal situation, I don't revert to my old habits. And once the rehearsals are going, I'll build on those to make sure that, when it's the concert, I'm just going to continue to do the same things. I'll be more nervous. A concert is always more anxiety, more nerves, more adrenaline. Not all of that is bad, it gets me more pumped up. But there is more opportunity for getting too much adrenaline."

Well then, just go back to Centering.

"So I can use tomorrow to practice for the rehearsal and the rehearsals to practice for the concert."

And use the concert to practice for. . . .

"The audition!"

Exactly.

"I just need to keep at it."

I like what I'm hearing.

"Good!"

I'm going to try and get that Shostakovich piece so I know what you're playing.

"Oh, there are so many recordings. It really is a warhorse. One of the more popular ones, because it's such a great piece."

Well, good. I'll look forward to hearing it.

"I'll try to tape the broadcast. If I'm playing first on it and I have as good a performance as I think I'm going to have, that will be a keeper and I'll send it to you."

I'd enjoy that. Thanks. Well, Brian, it seems like you're right on track.

"Okay, well you just keep steering me in the right direction."

As I said goodbye to Brian, I was thinking about what we had talked about. His experience with Centering as a physical sensation as much as it was mental was an unusual reaction that seemed very effective for him. The visualization technique was a perfect combination with the Centering, in that it allowed him to build a positive mental outlook to match the internal focus strengthened through Centering. The integration of skills was finally coming together, and his improved performance attitude reflected this progress.

CHAPTER FIVE

Getting Better

SING IT AT A SEVEN

Unlike Brian, Veronica was still having difficulty finding her center consistently. She seemed to have less trust in herself than Brian had. At the same time, she was utilizing the process cues in a dynamic fashion, effectively changing them as the pieces took shape. Our next conversation focused on this ongoing sequence of breathing, Centering, relaxing, and focusing. This would involve a brand-new, rather unconventional tactic to put Veronica in the right frame of mind. It would also help her learn to trust the effectiveness of the entire process. But first, I asked her to bring me up to date on her progress.

"OK. I did the new addition to the breathing exercises, but it was hard to do. We talked about saying the words during breathing. . . ."

. . . with meaning and conviction.

"Right. I couldn't say them all with conviction and I couldn't immediately go to sitting up and doing it. I had to lay down to do it for a while. But then I started getting better and better."

That's the practice.

"So that went well. I didn't have time to begin singing the first part of each piece. I had time to do it with only one song. But what was interesting was the way that I would sing it with the cue words. It would be the way that I would sing it when I'm practicing. Maybe having the cue words will help me to do the same thing in an audition. I always wondered, 'How come I have the courage to sing it like this by myself, but I never have the courage to sing it this way in an audition?' Why is that?"

Good question! Tell me more about that.

"Well, because during difficult vocal sections, you can't back away from it. There is a chance that you can crash and burn, but pulling away from it is not going to make it any better. It's just going to make it very weak."

Yes.

"But when I'm practicing, there's absolutely nothing at stake, so I can be vulnerable and risk making a big mistake because I'm by myself. But in auditions, I won't be able to do that extrastrong thing, particularly in this one. I'm talking about the *Carmen*, where you just have to do it. You just have to have a lot of strength singing it. The end part's very difficult."

Wait, wait. Let me write that down. *Carmen* . . . end part difficult. We will come back to this. Tell me more.

"Well, I had to change my cue words on one song."

To what?

"Can I use the word 'focus'?"

On which one?

"On the lighter Rossini. 'Words' just didn't do it for me."

Good. You're finding cues that you can say with meaning and conviction, not sarcastically.

"Yeah, right, right. So instead of 'in control,' I just used 'control,' and that worked."

Wonderful! You're moving along. What else?

"I'm trying to get a better sensation of where my center is and being able to visualize it. And a couple of times when I did the breathing exercises, when you open your eyes and project your voice out to a place, I was able to get the sensation of what that actually feels like; being able to do that and stay strong in my position."

And what's that feel like?

"Really good. It feels really solid."

Ahh. You're doing just great!

"And I've decided that I'm going to sing the lighter Rossini tonight and this weekend."

Perfect! Well, let's work today on just the light Rossini. Let it be a trial run-through, so you can get things working for you. So on the light Rossini, tell me the cue words again.

"They're 'focus' and 'control.'"

Define what you mean by 'control.'

"Basically I mean breath control. That I'm supporting every note I'm singing and that I'm keeping a steady tempo. Otherwise things can get very ugly." We both laughed.

"Plus it keeps me holding myself back that way in this piece. It makes me take the time I need with the music and with what's going on."

The holding yourself back?

"Yeah. I suppose that wouldn't be great for everybody, but since I get very overexcited and want to run up and sing it. . . ."

So holding back makes you more what?

"Umm . . . more calm."

Is there anything else I should know before we start?

"Oh, oh. I don't know! I don't think so!" She laughed.

Here we go, then. When you're either sitting down or lying down and you take your nine breaths, do the first three breaths help your muscles to relax?

"When I'm thinking about it, yes."

Well, when you're doing the three breaths, are you thinking about it?

"When I'm thinking 'inhale,' I think about my abdomen, and then on the exhale, I relax my neck and jaw. I realized how tense it was before I relaxed it."

Okay, then I want you to continue doing that on the first three breaths. On the next three, when you visualize being at your center, are you getting a better feel for being there?

"I think so. I usually visualize being at my center and also feel it at the same time. Is that okay?"

Do you feel like that's getting you out of your head and more focused on one point?

"Yes, definitely. Oh, and I can do it sitting up now."

Hallelujah! Way to go, Veronica!

"Thanks."

Okay. In terms of preparing for tonight's audition, would you like to stay with sitting down as opposed to standing?

"It doesn't matter. I can try it either way."

So today, you could practice Centering while you're standing and also try to cut back on the total number of breaths from nine to six.

"Oh . . . but tonight before the audition. . . ?"

Tonight, as long as they have a chair there, you could do it sitting down. I'm not recommending that you lie down.

"I've seen weirder things at auditions." She laughed.

Whatever feels comfortable to you. I'm fine with your sitting. And for tonight, if you need to take more breaths, please do so, so that you accomplish what you need in each sequence.

"Okay."

If you go there and it takes you four or five breaths to get your jaw relaxed, well then, take more.

"Oh, okay."

But stay there until you've accomplished it. And then the same thing with your center. If, because of stuff going on around you, it takes more than three breaths, then take more and stay there until you get there.

"I see."

The purpose of this is to make it work for you; it's not just to do a drill.

"Right, right."

So during the third sequence, on the first couple of breaths, think 'control,' and everything that it means to you. And then when you've got a good sense for 'control,' then move to 'focus.' And with that focus from your center, open your eyes and project it out through your voice to a point. Does that work for you?

"Yes. Yeah."

Now today, do that with the light Rossini and sing the entire aria.

"Okay."

Oh . . . I've got something else for you to do. You've got to trust me on this one. The reason why we're doing this is because you're going to feel some anxiety before you sing. I promise.

"Oh God." We both laughed.

Here's the drill. I hope you like this. [She laughed.] Do you live in an apartment?

"Yes."

What floor?

"Third."

Ahh, that's perfect. I would literally like you to set up a tape recorder, turn it on, leave your apartment and run up and down the stairs to get your heart going.

"Okay."

I'm not saying ten minutes, I'm just saying get your heart really going.

"In any way that I want?"

Any way that you want to do it. Then come back into the room with the tape recorder already going, and while your heart's still pumping, get centered and then sing the light Rossini all the way through.

"Oh God! Okay. Let's see if I can calm myself down, basically."

Well, here's the thing, Veronica. Centering is a great, great tool, and you need to see how good it is and to learn to trust it. It's not going to drop your heart rate down dramatically, but it will help. And besides, we don't want to take away all the energy that you could put into your voice.

"Right."

So we're not going to wipe it out. We're just going make it more under your control. Start to practice having it work for you. So today, get your heart rate up, use the Centering to get you to a better place, and then sing your best. That's the drill.

"Okay."

I want you to start using it so you can feel it work. Tonight at the audition, you won't have to run up and down the stairs to get your heart going.

She laughed. "No, it'll probably just be there."

If we took it on a scale from one to ten, with one being very frightened and ten being extremely courageous, would you say that at home, you can sing that at a nine or a ten?

"Uh . . . yeah, I can."

And what are you normally in performance situations?

"Probably around a five."

I wouldn't ask you to sing it in public right now at a nine or a ten, but what about a seven?

"Hmm. Seven would be something. If I sang it at a seven at an audition, I would be proud of myself."

When you're practicing today at home, with the tape recorder on, sing it at an eight and see what it sounds like. Then tonight, cut it back a notch and sing it at a seven. I'm not asking you to sing it at a nine or a ten at the audition, but a five is more dangerous than a ten.

She laughed. "I hate five. Five is just wimpy."

Being overcautious is no help. You are going to be exposed out there. You might as well let it out.

"Okay."

So I want you also playing with that today. Try and get to an eight and watch what it does and then cut it back for tonight.

"So I'm just going to work on the lighter Rossini today. I'll practice the Centering and take the amount of breaths I need."

Make it work for you. Can we talk tomorrow morning? I'll want to hear how it went and I'll have a few other things for you to do.

"I'm sure you will!" We both laughed. "Alright. I'm excited. I can't wait to sing tonight."

While Veronica was learning how to use her courage and trust herself more, Brian was figuring out how to trust his surroundings. He was getting a better grasp on his energy while performing, but it was now time to focus on his concerns about his success and failure. Outside pressures—the audience, judges, and so on—can be just as harmful as the internal ones, as you will see.

JUST "POST-IT"

I spoke to Brian about a week later, but I didn't get it on tape. He told me that the Shostakovich went well. He had used the three Centering breaths, and it worked. He said that he was even considering volunteering to play the Shostakovich again that evening. We agreed to talk the following week. I asked him to practice condensing the number of breaths he took in order to center. He was on his way to a long road trip. He called the following Monday.

"Hi, Don. I think you'd be pretty proud of me. I played the long road gig and played very well. A very hot, dry stage, and I still had a good one. And then the big test, I thought, was yesterday. It was a home concert. I was a little more apprehensive than I had been for the road concerts. I had written down in my training diary, 'Am I going to screw up this time?' I thought maybe it was because I was home and here it was the fourth one."

But you didn't.

"And another thing that I've noticed about me is that when it's a big hall and you can see the balconies, I have a thing about 'peering eyes.' Like all the tension's focused on me, as unrealistic as that might be most of the time, except during that big solo, then everybody knows who's really playing. So that got me a little more anxious, but I did all my focusing and everything and I played really well. The brass section got bows every concert. But the conductor gave me the first solo bow and the crowd just exploded."

That's great!

"And so did the orchestra. So I felt really good about that."

Good for you.

"So it was a successful, eye-opening excursion. I was actually starting to enjoy it most of the time."

Aren't you supposed to enjoy it?

"Yeah, but not always. It's easy to enjoy on fourth horn, when there's less pressure."

So please bring me up to date about condensing the three breaths, and what kind of results you had.

"Yeah, I was able to do it right before the solo this time, when I was a little more anxious. I had been practicing with just one breath in, focusing and then putting my Ki out.

It wasn't totally successful, but it was pretty good. It steadied me down enough. I found that when I've got a long stretch and then a solo entrance coming up, if I just concentrate on my breathing and listen to what's being played, rather than thinking, 'Here it comes, twenty bars away,' and getting that feeling of impending doom, I do much better. It's not that bad, but it's anxiety, certainly. I would focus on my breathing and sometimes it was difficult to do, but I kept with it. I used to get what I'm sure was the onset of an anxiety attack, and I felt dizzy, like I was going to fall off my chair. A little bit of a panic reaction. I felt an inkling of that, but it was very brief and I just stayed with it and said, 'Nope, it's not going to get any worse. Just breathe.' I shouldn't say that I fought it off, instead I just let it 'float' away. I did have a momentary feeling of, 'Oh God, not this old thing again!' That was right at the beginning, and I was able to move it off to the side, out of my way."

That's very good.

"And Bob showed up a couple times and I just told him to go away. Boy, that's really one of the best things. You know, it's like, 'Is this going to be the time you miss that first G fortissimo entrance?' I told Bob to get out of here and maybe come back some other time. But he's the only one I've dealt with so far. I think I need to name those 'peering eyes.' . . ."

Sounds like a smart idea.

"I looked at some old notes and I know I feel more comfortable alone in a dark hall. And yet, in the same hall I feel differently when I know that there are people listening, that there are 'peering eyes' out there, and it's really silent, and you're making almost the only noise. That's something I think I could put my energy toward dealing with and releasing. Letting it go."

What's a good way to reframe that?

"Well, I think that the peering eyes are a form of judge. There's somebody out there who has heard me play and is saying, 'Maybe he's going to screw this one up,' or something like that."

So it's the peering eyes of judges?

"I believe so. And obviously I don't feel that if I'm in the hall alone. It's when it's a concert and not a rehearsal. It's not peering eyes of people on stage with me, it's those in the audience sitting out there. And I think that stems from when I was in my school days at Northwestern. We'd go to hear the Chicago Symphony all the time and listen intently. And of course, they'd rarely miss. So now it's reversed and now I'm on stage. I know there are people out there like me, very attentive and listening for every little mistake. So I think that's where some of my anxiety from peering eyes comes from. Reversing that role."

So they're like mirrors?

"That's a good way to put it. Well, maybe not a mirror so much as knowing that those kind of people are out there. I've seen people with binoculars and figure they're watching me. So maybe I need to name that feeling, and hopefully it will be as effective as telling Bob to chill. I should find a good name. Bob works really well because it's short and sounds kind of funny."

Pick some different ones, use two or three.

"So I should come up with two to three names for the peering eyes?"

Yes. Like Fred, Mary, and Tom.

"Fred and Ethel. They'd make it a pairing. Fred and Ethel . . . or Lucy and Desi."

Whatever you want, as long as you deal with them like you've been doing with Bob. It would take the harsh edge off.

And besides, they might not even be listening. And then you can forget them.

"Okay. So they're watching me. And they're judging, but then I forget about them. I get over the feeling soon after the start, because the first entrance is quite a bit into the piece, and there are a number of different emotions, and then I come in with the theme. I did it better and better every night. I didn't miss the first note, even though that's one of the bugaboos. Like, 'What happens when you miss that note?' Because there are many famous orchestra pieces that start with horn. Those always scared me. It's like, 'Oh God, how do you do that?' That used to happen. I'd feel that everybody was watching and I'd feel the pressure. Not that I'd feel my legs heading for the door, but I would definitely be a little light-headed."

That was a normal part of your development.

"So feeling extreme anxiety was part of my development?"

Yeah. And you've progressed a lot since then, right?

"Oh, yeah!"

But part of you can still experience an adrenaline rush or quick shot of energy in certain circumstances. I can't guarantee that you won't feel that. But you've learned how to deal with that better.

"Definitely."

And you're going to learn even better. But the energy shouldn't be completely wiped away; it's not necessarily bad.

"Nerves are okay?"

Once that feeling stops, it's time to retire and move on to something you really care about.

"So that shows that I care?"

Yeah!

"That I want to do a good job. There's never a doubt that I want to do a good job."

Could you think about reframing that shot of adrenaline? It could remind you of the good old days or of all the distance you've come since then.

"Could you explain what you mean by 'reframing'?"

Instead of feeling the anxiety and saying, 'Oh, shit! That's just what I felt back then,' or 'I hope I don't make a mistake now,' it's feeling that anxiety and saying, 'Yup, I've learned how to deal with that.'

"So when I get that feeling . . . ?"

Don't interpret it as a bad or foreboding thing but just as a reminder of how far you've progressed since then.

"Okay, so when I get that feeling, I interpret it and say, 'There it is, my old friend.' How about that? 'My old friend.' I like that. So I interpret the feeling as my old friend and then acknowledge how far I've come in dealing with him."

Something like that.

"And this can be in conjunction with my breathing. I could be there, Centering my breath and thinking, 'Yeah. There's my old friend again. He's still with me, maybe he always will be, but I can control him.' I have proven that time and time again."

And that's what we'll call reframing.

"It's always going to be there. It's a part of me."

Well, it'll be less and less of a consequence. You can't necessarily erase it out of your existence, but you can deal with him and then let it go. Like waving to an acquaintance that's walking on the other side of the street. You just don't have any time for him, so it's just a 'Hey, how are you doing? Like 'See you later' kind of thing.

"And I could do this same kind of thing before these concerts. I haven't been totally worrying about it, but I know where I've had a big piece coming up, I won't be living quite as much. I'll be thinking, 'Maybe I'd better not do this because I've got this concert tonight. I'd better not go for a long bike ride.' Sometimes it bothers me. Certainly I wouldn't go off, not warm up and go take a trip and come back with ten minutes before the concert, but the other extreme would be to sit in the house and practice all day and fret, take a nap and worry about everything that could go wrong. I'm not at that extreme either."

Could you find a balance between those two?

"Yeah, I would like to find a balance. And sometimes I do and sometimes I don't. This was a new experience. If I'd been playing fourth horn instead, I know it wouldn't produce nearly as much anxiety. But if I had a solo engagement, if I were going to play a Mozart concerto, you'd better believe I'd be even more anxious than I was for the Shostakovich. And I know that's not a bad thing necessarily."

You're making a lot of progress, and it's starting to work well for you.

"Yeah. I really like the Centering technique. Okay, now I'd tentatively like to name the 'peering eyes' Fred and Ethel."

Or you can come up with other ones.

"Okay. I'll come up with something good."

Just acknowledge them and say, 'Thanks for coming to watch.' They're some of your old friends, so realize how far you've already come.

"Right, and it's not going to get me. I'm not going to go screaming off stage or fall off my chair. I know that I can play well with that kind of feeling because I did it four times in a row."

Exactly. And that doesn't guarantee ninety-nine times out of a hundred, or a hundred out of a hundred, but we'll get to that ninety-six repetitions from now. Okay?

"Uh huh. So it was a good week."

Tell me your schedule, Brian.

"Well, I wanted to talk to you about my Houston prep, which I got a good start on today. I really want to firm up Houston. I almost have two hours in today and I'm not done yet. I've been going through my old practice notes, and there are technical exercises I need to do; to keep up my trills, my slurs, multiple tonguing. Things that I should be doing. I just played through some of the cello suites. My chops, with my confidence and the work that I've been doing, everything's working really well. I want to apply that energy toward the Houston list. And that's not my only chance, because San Francisco's coming up, and that's another job I would have a very good shot at. So Houston is not my last chance. I've taken a hard look at it. I definitely want Houston, but if it doesn't happen, I'm not going to kill myself!"

Think in terms of preparing yourself the best you can for it.

"Yeah. Maybe you could give me a little impetus or help me with something. I went through about half the list, just went through the excerpts one after the other and they all were going pretty well. A couple of them are still giving me trouble, though. I think I ought to redo my list of ones, twos and threes."

That would be great.

"Okay, so redo that. Should I keep it to three, or did you like having that subcategory between one and two?"

Whatever works for you. Either way is fine. It's important to put them in separate categories, but think of the threes in terms of challenges or opportunities.

"Maybe the threes should receive my highest priority right now?"

How about the twos and threes.

"So I don't practice those things I'm already good at. Just play the challenging ones."

And come up with a positive thought for each one of them. Like. . . .

" . . . I can play this better than anyone."

Well, come up with a word or phrase for each excerpt on your threes list, with the same power that was behind that one.

"So assign a unique word. . . ."

. . . and in your mind, put a 'Post-it' note on each excerpt. So you would put the 'I can play this better than anyone' note on that last piece of music. Then when you think of that piece or when you put it on your music stand, that's what you'll hear and see in your head.

"So when I put that excerpt up and it comes into my visual range, that 'Post-it' note with that phrase or word is just there, boom! front and center, as if it were attached right there, and then I play whatever that evokes for me."

Try to do that this next week for all the twos and threes.

"And each one of those gets its unique word or phrase?"

Yes. I'd love to go through them with you next time we talk.

"Okay, so have the 'Post-its' ready for all the twos and threes for next time. Good! That is exactly what I need! I've even made a list of what I'm going to do in this period. I'm going to put together a tape of all the excerpts in the order that's on the list. That's something that I've been putting off. I need to get the music going. My playing is really good right now, but my prep is what needs work. This project is going to be enough right now, because I've got to play the licks and do a little soul-searching to find just the right phrase or word for each of them."

That's great! When can we talk again?

"Next week. Monday is good. How about seven o'clock?"

Fine.

"Okay, I'll call you at seven and have the list. I won't have any concerts to tell you about because I don't have any for a while."

Just put yourself in those situations of playing those pieces in auditions.

"Yeah. Go to the mental movies. I got it."

Both Veronica and Brian were now in the heart of the entire process. Both had the ability to put themselves in that stress-filled mind-set with the intention of controlling the energy through Centering, visualization, and role playing. The important thing to remember is that performance anxiety is not something to alleviate entirely but something to utilize in a more controlled, active manner that can actually improve performance. By personifying those peering eyes and befriending them, or by using high energy to invoke new life into a piece, Veronica and Brian were making their anxiety actually work for them rather than against them.

CHAPTER SIX

Courage

OPTIMAL PERFORMANCE

Learning how to feel more comfortable with the nerves and energy that accompany performing sounds counterintuitive, especially to someone like Veronica, who was still struggling to trust her own performance strategy. This often indicates a lack of courage, and it was time to show Veronica how anxiety can actually be transformed directly into courageous action. No performance can be 100 percent perfect, but one done with courage and focus can win the audition with flying colors. My next conversation with Veronica the following morning touched upon both of these critical points. First, I wanted to know how her audition went.

"It was very interesting. I was able to do everything vocally that I wanted to do."

That's wonderful!

"And I was very courageous. It was very interesting! I was still nervous."

I told you that you would be.

"Yeah, I was still really nervous and it was so strange, because usually in an audition I kind of go into another part of my brain and just . . . I don't know what I do! Yet I didn't do that last night. Part of it was hard because I couldn't really act. I was able to stand in one place and breathe really well and do all the vocal things I wanted to do, but I wasn't able to act as much."

We haven't talked about acting.

"Right!" We both laughed. "But I've never done that. Well, I shouldn't say never, but I've very rarely gone to an audition and been able to sing the way I sing at home. And I feel like I did. And I won five hundred dollars."

So what's the bad news?

"I don't think there is any bad news. But I was so nervous I was going to cancel it."

I would have shot you.

"I know you would have! That's why I didn't." She laughed. "So I went."

Was the nervousness down a little?

"Well, I think it would reach the same amount, but it came down when it was time to sing. Once I started singing, it was not an issue. But before that. . . ."

Before you go on, you should get nervous. If you're flat, if you don't get nervous, it's time to look for something else that will be important to you. Our goal is not to get rid of your nervousness. It's just to not have it affect your singing. But you're going to feel it.

"Oh, good. Because I thought, 'Oh gee . . . what's wrong?' I'm still nervous."

What I'd love to do is tie it to your courageousness.

"Yeah. Okay."

So what I'd like you to do with that is, when you feel nervous, let that remind you to be courageous. Because you are going to feel nervous.

"Right."

And just say, 'Yup, I've been here before. I've done this before. I'm going to be courageous.' Okay?

"Okay."

So we're going to tie the nervousness to courageousness. Because you're going to feel that, but the idea is to use your courage to work your way past your fears. Take me back to yesterday and to your running up and down the stairs.

"Yeah, I did that. Ran up and down the stairs, ran around the apartment."

Did that get your heart going?

"Yeah."

Did that mimic, a little bit, some of what you feel at an audition?

"Yeah, it did. Because at least I got the shallow breathing part. And I think I took about fifteen breaths and then I was ready to sing."

And how did you sing?

"Okay! I kept stopping, though."

Stopping what?

"Whenever I would do something I didn't like, I would go back and do it again. So I don't know if that really counts, instead of just singing it through. I stopped and fixed things and changed it."

Okay. Did we talk about perfection at all?

"Yeah, I think we did. That was one of those first things that we talked about a little bit in the first session."

Oh, yeah. I need to define a term for you, and the term is 'optimal.' I'm not sure what it means to you, but let me explain what it means to athletes. Everybody going into a pressure situation, whether it's an audition or the Olympics, is going to feel pressure. That pressure is going to affect them in either a minor way or a major way, but it's going to affect them.

"Right."

Probably ninety-nine out of one hundred of them will not do as well under that pressure as they're used to doing in less-pressured situations, namely in rehearsals or in practice or at home. It just doesn't work that way. Because they're under pressure, they're not going to be as sharp, as good, as relaxed, or as focused. So then we bring in the word 'optimal.' And 'optimal' simply means that, given that they're nervous, given that they're feeling pressure, given that people are watching them, given that they know it's important and there are consequences, they're not going to nail it. The best they'll do is 'optimal'—namely as good as they can, given the circumstances.

"I see."

But it's certainly not perfection. The one who wins either the audition or the Olympics is not the person who performed perfectly. That rarely happens, and it's just out of the question. The one who wins either the Olympics or the audition is the one who makes the least number of bad mistakes.

We both laughed.

"Right."

And what we're working on is not getting you to sing perfectly. It's getting you to sing as well as you can, given that you're feeling nervous. Does that make sense?

"Yeah."

But we're not striving for perfection, or to get you singing the way you do at home. We're trying to get you to sing as well as you can in an audition. And given how we're going so far, that's going to be better than everyone else.

"Oh, good!"

So that's what we're going to call 'optimal.' We're going to always strive for 'optimal,' never perfection. So when you're feeling nervousness, you'll now have a strategy to use. Yes, you'll still feel nervous, your performance won't be perfect, but it should be your best, given the circumstances, which should be better than everyone else because they don't know this stuff.

"Right."

And before Saturday I'm not going to tell any of them.

"Great!" We both laughed.

So when you did do the running and you got your heart rate up and then went through the breathing, did you feel then that you were at least in a better position, in more control, somewhat calmer, than if you hadn't?

"Yes. At the beginning I don't think I could have started. I mean, I could have started singing, but it would not have been very good. But by the end, I could sing."

Great, because that's what we're going to keep on doing. I hope you like your stairs. (laughs)

"Oh, I need a couple more flights, though. I'll have to go down twice."

Whatever it takes. Go outside or whatever. I'm serious. The key thing is to get your heart rate up. And I don't care how you do it. Just so you get it up. Are you used to taking your heart rate?

"Uh, yeah. I used to do it a lot."

Okay. I want you to start doing it. How do you do it?

"Let's see. Either 15 seconds or 30 seconds on my wrist."

I want you to keep on doing it. Do you know what your heart rate is for one minute?

"Something around 70."

Okay. Here's what I'm going to ask you to do. I want you to start keeping track of it and certainly get it up to 90 or 100.

"Okay."

And then when we start doing audition run-throughs, I'm going to ask you to do it then too. I just want you to get used to it. Let's say you run up and down your stairs in your apartment and you get your heart rate to 100. Then you do your breathing and bring it down, and you sing well. Well, then before you go into the audition and you feel your heart pumping, I'm going to want you to feel your pulse and say, 'Yeah, it's 100. I've been practicing at 100.'

"Oh, yeah. I see. Oh, good."

Because it's the same. And it really doesn't matter whether you get it up from running up and down stairs, or just from walking into an audition. It's the same response and you're going to have the same solution.

"Okay. Great!"

So the Rossini piece went well?

"Yeah!"

Super. Let's move to the other pieces and do the same thing. How long are those pieces? How many minutes?

"Oh God ... *Carmen* is a little over two minutes. The Rossini is probably four minutes, and the Bernstein four minutes as well."

Is there a place where you can go, like a rehearsal hall or studio, where you can just go in and just sing?

"Hmm. No. I don't think so."

Is there any place outside of your apartment where you sing?

"Just in lessons and with coaches and auditions."

Do you think you could find a place that's convenient?

"That's not in my apartment?"

Yes.

"Yeah, I could at someone else's house. Does that count?"

Sure. Please check into that, because your place is very comforting, it's security. I want to get you out of there, but not for the stuff that we're doing. I want you to keep on practicing there. But I would love you to set up a situation. Let me just give you an example. At a friend's house, at seven o'clock, tell that friend, especially if it's a singer or a musician, that you'd like to come over and go through your songs.

"Ooooooo...."

Yeah.

We both laughed.

"Okay. They don't have to watch or anything, do they?"

Not the first night. [laughs] Veronica, I'm going to keep on putting pressure on you because there's nothing I can do about the pressure that's going to be put on you at the audition, other than preparing you for it and teaching you how to deal with it. But listen, you can do it.

"Oh, yeah. Yeah. Alright."

Courage is like a muscle. You strengthen it by using it.

"I like that."

So I'm just going to raise the bar.

"I'm ready for the next level."

Try to set that up. Not necessarily for tonight but certainly by Wednesday or Thursday.

"Okay."

I want you to start bringing the number of breaths down. I'm not going to put a number on it, I just want less. But I don't want you leaving any one of the segments until you've done it. In other words, don't move on until your neck and jaw are relaxed. But we'll try to get that to be in fewer breaths.

"Okay."

And then don't move on until you're really at your center.

"Okay."

Did you feel more focused last night?

"Yeah, I did. Well, basically I felt more like I was really in control. I felt like I'm the one that's deciding how this piece is going to be. Not the piano player. It's me, and I can take my time where I want to take my time."

Wow! That's wonderful!

"Yeah! That's what I felt. Focused? I think I might have to change that because I was using that as one of cue words. I don't know.... I think it might be too vague for a cue word."

Good. Keep on refining it.

"Yeah. I'll just find something else."

And we're going to keep on refining it. These cue words won't be the same for the next twenty years. We're going to use them and eventually they'll wear out. They'll have no meaning to you; you'll just be mouthing the words. And that's when it's time for us to move on. So we'll be continually finding new words. And your singing's going to change. What you need now, you may not need a month from now. You may need something else.

"Wow!"

So always be looking for the right words to take in with you. Plan ahead of time.

"Okay. So in other words, I don't want to be sitting outside the audition thinking, Now is it 'control' or is it 'focus' or ...?" We both laughed.

So did you do the breathing sitting or standing before you went in?

"I did it sitting."

Okay. I want you to start transitioning to standing. Did you put the tape recorder on yesterday?

"Yeah."

I meant to tell you, I don't necessarily want you listening to it.

"Oh good. I listened to parts of it."

I don't want you chopping it up. But again, that's just another source of pressure.

"Yeah, it is, actually."

Again, I'm going to keep on asking you to take on more pressure and then deal with it. So more standing than sitting. Fewer breaths as opposed to more. Keep on looking for good cue words. Have you found good cue words for the Bernstein piece yet?

"Um. Not really."

I want you to, okay?

"Okay."

So that's your first assignment. The next one is to get your heart rate up with the tape recorder on, come back in and sing one piece all the way through without stopping.

"Okay."

Then do two pieces all the way through without stopping, and then three pieces all the way through without stopping. And that may take you a day or two to get through, but I want you to go through all three pieces without stopping.

"Okay. Oh, wow!"

Yeah, I know. Again, I don't want it to be, 'Well, I'm just at home and nobody's listening, so I can stop.' I want you working through it.

"Okay. I have another audition on Thursday night."

Wonderful! And then, after you do the three, I'm going to start asking you to switch them around. But I'm also going to want you to go through the Bernstein piece.

"Okay."

Do you know what you're going to be singing at the audition on Thursday night?

"I figured that I'd start with the serious Rossini."

Oh, good. Same pieces then?

"Same pieces exactly."

Good. Can we talk Thursday morning?

"Yeah!"

Good. Because you're doing great.

"I am?"

You're right on track. You've got to trust me. You're really right on track.

"Well, I was so relieved after last night because part of the nervousness was because of this weekend. But you can't ignore these feelings and just hope that they're going to go away."

No, Veronica, they're going to be there.

"Yeah."

They're just not going to affect your performance. But they're going to be there, I promise you.

"Uh huh. All right. Oh good!" She laughed.

I'm sorry. If you don't want the nervousness, get out of opera.

"I love it, though!"

And that's part of the reason you're nervous. It's because you do love it and you want to sing well. Questions?

"Uh, nope. I've got to go to a friend's house and sing, keep doing that, do what I did with the Rossini yesterday, and do that with my other pieces. I'll be busy."

Yes. Get the breathing down, do it standing, go through the pieces with no stopping, and find a friend's house to use.

"Okay. I'll do that tomorrow. Okay!"

All right. You just keep up the good work. You're doing great!

We ended our conversation after having covered a lot of ground, but as you can see, all of these techniques were geared toward one ultimate goal—a courageous and focused performance. Learning how to control her heart rate quickly and effectively in strange places allowed Veronica to deal better with the anxiety-ridden environments of auditions, and easing her obsession with perfection lowered the bar just enough to allow for an expressive, confident performance.

PUT YOURSELF ON THE SPOT

Brian was also struggling with confidence issues, but these seemed more on his inability to play well consistently. In the following conversation, we discussed his strategic approach to each excerpt, and went further into the value of practicing in foreign environments, including even the audition location. But first, Brian brought me up to speed on his recent work.

"I've made really good progress on a number of excerpts, including the category threes."

In terms of practice?

"In terms of practice, it's been an extremely productive week. And in terms of life in general, I got a lot of things done. I got some good bike-riding in, and I'm playing really well."

Did you start using the 'Post-it' notes?

"Yeah. I definitely have the list established with the ones, twos, and threes. As a matter of fact, I've been shifting a few of them around. I moved one up to the second and one back down to the third, because I was pissed at it. But as far as the mental 'Post-it' notes go, were they supposed to be a word or phrase that describes how I feel about the piece or what I want to do with it?"

You can start with whatever first comes to mind with an excerpt.

"So for like Beethoven's *Seventh* allegro excerpt, I just put 'springtime,' because it reminds me of springtime. And for the Beethoven *Seventh* trio, it's a 'relaxed lilt' underneath the nice woodwind melody. But for most of these, I couldn't come up with a very good label. Maybe I missed what you were driving at."

The specific label is not the important thing, it's just a starting point. But especially for each excerpt in the third category, you need to come up with a process cue that captures how you play when you play it well.

"I do have cues for almost all of them. Only two aren't named. There are six total in category three. The only thing I don't have named is the Haydn *Double Concerto*, because I don't know the piece at all. It's in category three because I've never worked on it."

What are some of the words or phrases you have for some of the other threes?

"Well, for the Beethoven *Ninth*, I have 'tranquil and confident.' And for Strauss's *Heldenleben*, 'crisp and menacing.' How's that?"

Is that you or the piece?

"Both. There's a certain part of it that should be crisp, and it is menacing. But I found I played an audition round today and I just pulled numbers out of a hat. I wound up playing three of the six category threes on the list and I stank. No way to play an audition. But I learned a couple of good things. I tried to overplay the one that's crisp and menacing, and that's before I named it. So I'm trying to be crisp and menacing, rather than overpowering with it. Crisp is not like a sledgehammer."

So when you bring that piece out and it captures your attention, the thought of 'crisp and menacing' should come to mind.

"And that's the mental 'Post-it' note that I will attach to it. Yeah, for the opening of the Mahler *First Symphony*, I have 'warm, thin air stream.' That's certainly different from 'spring-time' or 'crisp and menacing.' Is that more of a process cue or is there no difference between those two?"

They're similar, and both of those are fine.

"The 'relaxed lilt' sets me up to play that well, because one of my teachers said, 'You know, it's a relaxed excerpt. Don't try and blow the crap out of it.' That's sometimes my tendency. For the Tchaikovsky *Fourth*, I have 'rhythmic intensity' because, again, he told me that this is not a lick that you're supposed to blow the crap out of. They want to hear the intensity and the drive out of the rhythm. They want to know that you can stay consistent with the rhythm and know how the tune goes."

Good. Did you come up with any others?

"I think I only have a quarter of them named. Actually, the ones I haven't named in category three are page-long excerpts, and I'm preparing to play the whole page. For the *Don Quixote*, I said 'storm-swept rocks' because it's two excerpts, two variations from *Don Quixote*, and one uses a wind machine in back of the percussion. And the other one is a rising and falling melodic line, and I haven't come up with a good name for that yet."

Okay.

"For the *Rheingold* excerpt, I came up with 'smooth waves,' and I've been working on a glissando technique that a friend of mine told me about. It's a lot better, but it's still going to stay in category three."

How about your Centering exercises?

"I've been doing them, and although I haven't had the pressure situations to try it out, I did the full boat. I jogged in place and thought all these negative thoughts, and then calmed myself down and came in and played like crap."

Why was that?

"Because they were excerpts that I wasn't playing well. And it was in the morning, right about the time when I'll be playing, about two weeks from today. But it didn't concern me that much."

So then make sure that you put that into your routine every day.

"As a matter of fact, I have another list. I have a short and a long list that I want to do every day. The long list is more like a semifinals list."

How are the images in your head of how it's going to go?

"As far as going to the movies about Houston?"

Yes.

"I've not done much of that."

OK.

"I think I'm just about to start, though. I used this last week to kind of get me going, to get a practice routine established and work on the excerpts. I've made progress on a lot of them. Of the excerpts I've played so far, *Fidelio* was perfect and the other Beethoven went pretty well, and the Tchaikovsky *Fourth* was pretty good. I haven't listened to the tape yet. I did it this morning and I let it sit for a while. So I'm going to come back to that tonight before I do my long list. Yeah, I need to start and I'm going to be playing for a friend on Wednesday, so he'll just run me through my paces."

Super!

"One of my concerns is that I did this before Detroit, playing really well, and then I seemed to ramp down about a week before, in intensity and in playing level. And by the time I got to Detroit, I was definitely in a trough. The way I was for Detroit was the way I was last week. I mean, this last week I was just hot. I was playing everything. And I don't quite feel that now, but I do realize what I've done is probably reached another plateau."

OK.

"I think I've reached about three plateaus in the last two months, maybe even month and a half. My playing is really doing that kind of upward spiral. So I might be on another plateau. I'm not going to panic, but I would appreciate the benefit of your experience as far as peaking too early as opposed to peaking at the right time, because I really didn't do something right in Detroit. I felt mentally and emotionally unprepared. If I'd gone in the week before I would have won it, the way I was feeling. I don't want to do that again."

And you've got two weeks to go, right?

"Yeah. Two weeks from today."

Let's work through that together. The idea is to see yourself playing better and better and better.

"Yeah. That definitely has been happening."

And as long as you're not there with all the pieces in category three, just keep on moving forward.

"I've been working on the category threes and giving them a lot of attention."

That's great! And just keep on until they're all category ones.

"I was working on some category twos as well. And I don't want to forget about the ones either!"

Please do all three when you put yourself into the routine.

"So pull some out of each category?"

Yes.

"So what do you think could have caused me to peak early for Detroit and start the downward slide?"

I'm really not interested in dredging that up or setting you up so that it happens again. Let's just move forward.

"So there's no preventative maintenance needed to be done as long as I keep progressing?"

That's the idea.

"So, I had set some deadlines for myself to have everything named by Sunday and to have a tape of all the excerpts, neither of which I did. What I have been doing is some listening, and what I'll do tonight, as soon as we're finished, is play the Beethoven *Ninth*, the entire third movement at least twice, maybe three times. Just sit there in front of the stereo, play with the music, because I've got the whole part. This is just for pacing and just to feel comfortable, because I want to feel as tranquil and relaxed at the end as I did in the beginning. It's a long excerpt and I tend to get tension built up. So if I can do the whole movement a couple of times, whatever excerpt they throw at me, it should be that much easier."

Why don't you do that, and if you do anything other than nail it, let's talk about it in a few days.

"The Beethoven in particular?"

Yeah. If there's anything we need to discuss, let's get to it then.

"So what I'll do is treat it as a performance. I'll sit there before I cue up the tape and take my three breaths. I hadn't been practicing that as much, because I hadn't been at rehearsals or anything. I've been off."

The other thing you might want to do is figure out some different places to put yourself in performance situations.

"So I should do more mental movies?"

Well, not only more mental movies, but physically do it. I'm not saying you should rent a rehearsal hall, but if you could stay fifteen minutes after a rehearsal or go there half an hour early and put yourself in a different physical circumstance, and put yourself on the spot to play.

"Oh, I see. How about if I'm standing backstage before rehearsal and people are warming up and stuff and I'm doing an excerpt or two. People are always listening. That's somewhat of a pressure situation, because if you screw something up, people are going to hear. People are generally into their own routine, but that's a little bit of pressure."

Yes.

"And then treat that with the same Centering techniques?"

Exactly.

"Or I could play backstage during breaks. I do that anyway, but I haven't done that specifically. Okay, I'll get there early on Wednesday. We've got a double rehearsal on Thursday, so I'll plan to do a couple of those before, during and after both of the doubles."

Great!

"And I'll play every note. I'm planning ahead of time. I'm going to go in and produce these beautiful sounds and everybody's going to go, 'Wow.'"

There you go!

"I'm just going to make sure that I'm playing my absolute best, and we'll just see what happens in Houston."

Why don't we talk toward the end of the week?

"Okay. I've got a concert on Friday, but I could call you before, at six-thirty."

That would be great.

"Okay. So I'm playing for a friend on Wednesday. I've got a double on Thursday and I've got a rehearsal and a performance on Friday, and two performances on Saturday. I've got a lot of opportunities. But I don't want to overdo it, either."

Just keep taking forward steps, not worrying about plateauing or peaking early. Don't let that be a concern; we'll take care of it.

"The only reason I bring it up is not to try and be negative about it, but I know that I was putting in three-hour-plus days before the Detroit audition. I was doing the list maybe twice, maybe three times a day, pulling numbers out of a hat, and I thought I was really moving toward something. And it seems that I kind of burned myself out. I'm aware of that now, but I'm wondering where the fine line is, because I certainly went over it for Detroit."

Just keep moving forward. We have other things we're going to do.

"I didn't exactly take Sunday off, but I did more 'fun' practice and noodled in front of the TV, because I needed it. I really didn't want another hard day. And today I'm motivated. I've gotten good work in. I'm looking forward to getting to the Beethoven."

And I'll look forward to talking to you on Friday.

For Brian, courage meant confidence in consistent, ongoing progress. For Veronica, courage was having faith in her ability to sing her best at a given moment. At this point, both Veronica and Brian were using a very strategic system of practicing each piece or excerpt in order to build confidence through repetition and consistency. The changing process cues reflected their growing familiarity and awareness of the music, and each was learning how to bring each piece of the puzzle together to improve their overall control over performance.

Moving their practice sessions to unfamiliar locations raised the bar by placing them outside their comfort zones, just as an audition would do. After all of this, I had finally introduced the most critical element of performing—understanding that perfection is not the ultimate goal. Performing at your very best—your optimal level—is true success. Easier said than done? Well, this concept takes a while to sink in and comes up many more times in future conversations, but it is the key to audition success.

CHAPTER SEVEN

New Cues

FLOW

As the audition drew closer, Veronica was getting more and more excited. This is a typical, welcome response, for it brings the entire practicing routine even closer to the feel of the ultimate audition. Veronica's enthusiasm continued to be an asset, but I was interested to see how she was doing in lowering her revved up energy. This would be critical, especially when she was alternating between specific pieces.

"I'm getting a little bit hyper."

Good.

"I tried my resting pulse. Each day that goes by it increases."

That means you're getting ready for the audition. So bring me up to date on what you've been doing.

"Okay, let's see. I went over to my friend's house yesterday to sing some stuff, and it went pretty well. I did three of them, and actually went through the one that's been the hardest for me."

Is that the Bernstein?

"Yes. And it went pretty well."

You sound surprised.

"I know … well, that one went the worst, of course. But even at that, it's just that I'm not focused enough. It's not that it's actually not good, it's just that I don't know how to calm down during that piece yet. But the other pieces went very well and I was not really that nervous. All sorts of things started occurring to me that could go wrong, like 'Oh no, what if I can't do this?', or 'What if I can't do that?' But it all went okay."

What else?

"Let's see … I did my running around and got my pulse up to 120."

Wow!

"Is that a lot?"

That's a lot.

"I did jumping jacks. Then I did the breathing and got it down to an 86."

Veronica, that's fantastic! Magnificent! How many breaths did it take you?

"It took me one, two, three, four, five … ten. … I guess that's not so good."

That's fine.

"I wanted to make sure that I was relaxed, so I did as many as I needed."

That's the whole idea. It would be nice to take fewer breaths, but the goal is to get your heart rate down. If it takes a few more breaths to do that, it doesn't make that much difference right now. What's critical is getting your heart rate down, and it sounds like you're doing that.

"Then I sang through a couple of pieces and it was okay. It really is funny to do that in my apartment because I'm not used to having to be on edge like that in my own house. So it was, in a way, like being at an audition, because I wasn't as calm. But it went okay!"

[I laughed.] What else?

"Oh, the one thing that's been on my mind is that now I'm getting more nervous about them announcing the winners at the reception. I sing at eleven in the morning and the reception is at five-thirty. Everybody has to be there and they announce who they've accepted. So, having to deal with standing there and possibly not being accepted is really causing me a lot of stress."

Tell me more.

"I think it's because I don't really believe that I actually will be accepted. I'm thinking, 'Well, of course you're not going to be accepted. These good things just don't happen to you.' Isn't that awful?"

It's not awful, it's just not helpful. As the audition gets closer, it may get even more emphatic and louder. It's just part of your normal fears and doubts.

"Normal fears and doubts?"

So remember to keep your sense of humor.

"Okay. Did I tell you that I bought a new dress?"

For the audition or the reception?

"For the audition. So, if nothing else, I can wear my new dress on the stage of the opera house."

That's wonderful. So have you sung the Bernstein yet?

"Yes, I sang it yesterday."

And do you have your cue words?

"Argh! Well, I think I sing it best when I think about 'vowels.' Is that a cue word?"

That could be. What do you mean by "vowels"?

"Well, since it's in English, I think about the words too much and the consonants get in the way of the air going through—and that causes tension in my jaw. So if I just think about 'vowels'—I don't even know if that's going to work necessarily—but the idea is just to let the air through and let it flow."

I really like that! If that's what 'vowels' means to you, that's a great cue.

"Maybe I'll just write down what I just said. 'Flow.'"

Yeah, just letting it flow. Letting the air go through. That sounds great!

"Yeah, that is better than 'vowels.'"

Or just say 'vowels' and 'flow.'

"'Vowels' and 'flow.' That's good. Okay."

Now when you're practicing at home, after you get your heart rate up, start practicing with different pieces. How many did you say you were going to sing in Chicago?

"Well, I'll offer four, but most likely they'll pick two and I can pick the first one, so I can control it somewhat."

Have you picked that yet?

"Yeah, the lighter Rossini."

When do they tell you about the second piece?

"After I sing my first one, they deliberate and then they ask for the second one."

I'm going to ask you to make separate index cards for each of the other three pieces. On the cards, write the name of the piece and your cue words. Put them face down on the table by your tape recorder. Turn the recorder on, get your heart rate up, come back into the room, center, and get your heart rate down. Use the cue words for the lighter Rossini and then sing it. Then shuffle the other three cards, pick one, read the cue words and say them to yourself, and then sing the piece and nail it.

"That's great. That'll do it!"

As soon as you turn the card over, use the words to focus on what you need to do to sing it well. If you want to take a few breaths and center again, that's the time to do it.

"Okay, so I can take the amount of time I need?"

Yes.

"That's where I have the time pressure."

Then take two or three breaths. On the first one, focus on your neck and jaw. On the second one, be at your center. And on the third, think about your cue words and project that focused energy to a specific point. You'll have time to do that.

"Yeah, they'll wait."

Veronica, it's all of seven seconds.

We both laughed.

"Okay, good. Because then I have a plan for that time, instead of just floundering around and getting nervous."

You've got it! So how's your courage doing?

"Good! The voices, the 'what ifs,' tried to do some damage yesterday, but they didn't. I still did what I needed to do. When I was singing, they were sure trying. But even with some vocal things that didn't work, I still did them anyway with a lot of courage. I said, 'No! I'm going to do it.' So even things that weren't perfect were okay, and I still went for it."

That's wonderful! Let's talk about some other positive things for you to focus on. Did you tell me you've already been to Chicago?

"I've been there once, when I was there for the initial audition."

Do you remember what the hall is like?

"Pretty much."

This is a good time for you to start imagining yourself backstage, a few minutes before you go on.

"That makes me nervous just thinking about it!"

You're going to be nervous, that's for sure. But as you're feeling that, mentally run through your Centering and your breathing. Then imagine yourself getting relaxed, focused and walking out courageously.

"Okay. And calmly."

And imagine yourself going through the first Rossini piece, singing it very well.

"So I'm not actually singing it, I'm just going through it in my mind?"

Yes, but try to fully experience what you'd be feeling. If that makes you nervous, then you've got a strategy: do your Centering. After your first piece, when you're waiting for them to announce the second, take two or three more breaths and then nail that piece. And after you've walked off, feeling very happy, imagine being congratulated at the reception.

"Oh, okay. All right!"

Olympic athletes carry it through to standing on top of the awards platform and having a gold medal put around their neck. It's the same thing. It can be very powerful, if you practice it.

"I'll try."

And then the next time you rehearse it, choose a different second piece. I'd like you to keep notes each time you do this, once or twice a day for the next few days.

"Okay, got it. Oh, by the way, I have an audition tonight at seven."

Oh really? This is great!

"It's not anything crucial."

You can use your mental rehearsal practice today to get ready for that.

"Okay."

I'd like to talk in the morning about how it goes tonight, so you can tell me the good news.

"Yeah, sure. Of course! They'll probably ask for more than one piece, but I'm going to start with the light Rossini so I can get the feel of starting with that. I wouldn't be surprised if they asked for a second piece. So I can practice doing the other breaths."

That's great, Veronica. One last thing. Between now and the time they tell you you've won on Saturday, I want you to keep unwavering and unfaltering confidence in yourself. Start with a mental set right now that's confident, positive, and courageous. Keep that focus tonight and then take that with you to Chicago and into the audition. And that's it. Just sing like you can tonight and show them what you've got.

"Okay. I'll call you tomorrow!"

Confidence and focus had become Veronica's guiding lights. By playing around with different variations of each song, Veronica was limiting the surprise factor of the audition. Focusing on staying relaxed and positive through the audition and beyond also strengthened her courage muscle. Brian, as you will see, was at a very similar point. His numerous excerpts, any of which could be called for in the audition, contributed to the same surprise factor that we needed to alleviate. In our next conversation, we discussed this, along with some fun visualization strategies. Brian was about to start "going to the movies."

CLEAN AND EASY

One week later I hear from Brian.

Hi Brian. How are you doing?

"I'm doing really well. I've got a concert tonight. I played for some friends on Wednesday and Thursday between rehearsals. They ran me through everything, over an hour of having me out there, and I played most of the stuff very, very well. One of them told me that I was forcing things; part of it may have been the room, but when I got on stage it was much better. I think that getting on stage is a big thing."

What do you mean?

"Well, it's bigger and I don't have to force it, because I have the sense that when I'm on stage, I carry just fine, but when I'm in a small room, sometimes things back up and you just try and use more air, and I end up forcing things. So just between Wednesday and Thursday, there was a major improvement."

In terms of what?

"In terms of concentrating, focusing. I played all the licks quite a bit better. I've been going into rehearsals prepared to play for what I call 'the audience and colleagues who may or may not be listening.' And after my first note, I wanted to make sure that everything was just crystal clear, and everything was really good. And I stayed; I played forty-five minutes after rehearsals. I've been playing on stage quite a bit and it's been good for me to stay after and play another forty-five minutes. That felt good too."

That's great!

"And playing in that big room helps."

Is the Houston audition going to be in a big room?

"It'll probably be on stage. If it's not on stage, I imagine it would be downstairs in this rehearsal room, which is not bad. I've played down there before and it's got really nice acoustics. Either way, I was able to visualize playing there and playing well."

Last time we talked about naming more of the excerpts.

"Yeah, there are still a few that just escape me, but I've concentrated on how to start each of them. I figured out how to start more precisely, how to give myself the best entrance, like a pole vaulter getting ready. I need something, not necessarily to pump me up, but just so that I get a good start. So I named about five or seven more. Some of the excerpts I just look at and I know how to start, some I don't. I only have ten out of the thirty-four that I haven't named yet, so I'm two thirds of the way there."

That's wonderful.

"Three of them are the Schoenbergs that I've played extremely well for my friends. My fellow musicians couldn't find anything wrong with them, but I found a few little flaws."

What did they like about them?

"They were clean. Clean and easy. Even though they were technical, I made them sound easy."

There are two good process cues: 'clean' and 'easy.'

"Yeah, I could label the three Schoenbergs that, because I feel the same way about all three of those licks. I could label them all 'clean and easy,' or 'clean and easy one,' 'clean and easy two,' something like that."

Or "clean and easy, one two three." Just put the 'Post-it' note on each excerpt.

"I've been kind of hit-or-miss as far as actually putting it there before I play an excerpt, whether it's for myself or for somebody else. I've got to do that more."

Here's the drill. Have someone just randomly pick out excerpts, lay them face down, turn on the tape recorder, leave the room, go through your routine and Centering, and then go back into the room with your horn.

"Do I need to have somebody else there?"

No, you can do this on your own. Just pick two or three from each of the categories, shuffle those, and put them on your music stand. When you turn one over and see what excerpt it is, mentally attach the note to it and experience the thoughts and feelings that go with it. As soon as you say or hear the cue, start playing your best. And then do that again with the next piece.

"Okay, so pick six or seven at random. I don't even know what they are before I go out of the room?"

Right.

"I turn the tape deck on, go out of the room and then come in and pick up the first one and look at it. I'll just say for example, 'Okay, Beethoven Nine' and automatically picture the 'Post-it' note up there, 'tranquil and confident,' and then start to play it."

And play as tranquilly and confidently as you can for the first thirty or forty-five seconds. Then once it starts flowing, put that piece down, pick up the next one and do it all over again.

"And this is a way of imprinting my process cues onto the excerpts, with the 'Post-it' notes? Okay, I like that drill. Yeah, and that's something that I could do after tonight's performance."

You can do this any time and it need not take all that long, because you're only going to be playing short segments, the beginnings of each of the pieces you select at random.

"Right. So in a way, I'm practicing how to start these excerpts, how to put myself in the best frame of mind."

I'd recommend that you do this for about ten minutes at a time. Then take a break and move on to something else. Or shuffle them and start again, so that you go through all sorts of different sequences.

"Yeah, I haven't done that in the last four or five days because I've been playing for other people. I know that burnout is bad, but I'm not burned out. I just don't want to go overboard with it."

So we need to keep it fresh.

"Yeah, that's the key—keeping it fresh."

This would be a good time to go through your visualizations.

"Uh huh. I have not been going to the movies as far as, 'Okay, I've got five minutes before I go into the room to play my audition,' but I do try to get myself nervous, thinking, 'Oh boy, this is it. I don't want to blow this.' I get myself psyched and then do the three Centering breaths and bring myself down."

Good! For the visualization of bringing your energy down, see yourself going into the room, turning to the first piece, whatever piece comes to mind, noticing the 'Post-it' note, seeing yourself starting and playing the entire piece well, and then moving on to the next excerpt.

"Okay, so when I go to the movies, I want to see myself walking in and playing perfect renditions of these excerpts."

See yourself playing your best through them, finishing well, and then walking off happy.

"So go to the movies for Houston, pick two or three excerpts, nail them, and walk off happy."

And then stop. Then the next time you do it—say, later in the day, at night or the next day—do four or five different pieces. By the time you're there, you'll have played every piece at least once, nailing all of them in your mind.

"That's a good way to go to the movies. I should do this every day. How about twice a day?"

That's ideal.

"Twice every day, maybe mid-morning and the other near bedtime. As a matter of fact, I should probably do that now, before I get dressed. I'm running out of time, but it should be a good one tonight. I actually get a speaking line. It should be pretty interesting."

Really?

"It's the Magic Circle Mime. It's really clever. Basically we come on, the conductor has been killed before the concert even started, and we've got this guy who paid to conduct the orchestra. So he gets to conduct the orchestra, but he also gets killed, and we have to find out who killed these two conductors. It's a lot of 'shtick,' and it should be very entertaining. The band is really into it."

Is this the whole orchestra tonight?

"Yup. It's the last Pops series of the season."

And what do you have on Saturday?

"A family concert as well in the morning, so even though it's going to be a beautiful day, I'm not going to get a bike ride tomorrow. I want to make sure that I get some good practicing in, since it's a double concert day. And a good way not to be too tired chopwise is to do this mental practice."

That's a nice shift.

"I've got my list out in front of me now and I still see these blank spaces that I've got to fill in with the process cues. Some of them I don't seem to need, but it couldn't hurt to have one for each of them."

So it's there if you need it.

"I imagine that any process cue is better than none at all. I was a little concerned about not having the proper one, that it might. . . ."

You're right. Having the proper one is not as important as just having one. You can change it anytime. You might come up with a better one in your visualization. The idea is to have fun and be creative. You can learn within there how to play better.

"Maybe I should make the session for the ones that I haven't named yet and see if something comes to mind."

Start with one of the named ones you like, and then add one or two of the other ones.

"Okay, so to get the ball rolling, do ones that I like the phrase of, the 'Post-it' note? Right?"

Yes.

"So I have these two mental drills. Well, I have one that's not as much mental, picking the excerpts and turning the tape deck on, doing my whole preaudition routine, then going in and applying the notes and then playing the pieces."

Making sure those phrases get you off to a good start, because after that you're pretty much on cruise control.

"Yeah, once I get things going, there's no stopping me."

So you're just going to rehearse getting the ball rolling, knowing that your skill and talent will take over after that.

"Yeah, my best auditions have been when I've started well and then my confidence builds with each excerpt."

That's the feeling to have in Houston with every excerpt: that with each one, you're saying—"Yeah! I can do this. I can nail this one." All right! You've got it. When can we talk again?

"We could talk maybe Monday or Tuesday. I can tell you how the weekend went. And I will fill you in on what the movies are like."

Keep in mind that we're still making some subtle shifts.

"Right. I'm not going to get stale. A lot of these licks I'm nailing physically, but I'd like to get them more solid mentally as well."

Which is what we're moving toward.

"Yeah, I can see that. That's good. Before I forget, I'm going to write all of this down. I've got to drill and go to the movies in Houston. That ought to give me plenty to do."

Play well tonight, Brian. I look forward to talking with you next week.

This was a critical stage for both Veronica and Brian. Each of their auditions would call upon everything from their process cues to staying confident and courageous throughout. But having learned how to Center and practicing it over and over again, this entire process was becoming old hat for them now.

CHAPTER EIGHT

Getting Close

TRUST

We were entering the home stretch. Although both Veronica and Brian had been in and out of various performances up to this point, each situation had allowed the two performers to integrate more and more of the skills we had discussed. At this stage, just as one needs to relax the day before a big audition or performance, it was time to show Veronica and Brian how to relax mentally while fine-tuning any lingering doubts. I heard from Veronica the next morning.

"Okay. So I did the things we talked about, rehearsing the whole thing in my mind."

How'd it go?

"Okay. . . ."

Okay or good?

"Parts of it were really good, but there are little parts of it that I really have to work on, like when I'm walking out. I had trouble with that one, just imagining myself walking out in a great, confident manner."

Stay with that.

"Argh! You know, I can picture myself walking out like, 'Hi! Hi! I'm here to sing!' and being very excited and hyper about it. But I don't want to do that. I just want to walk out in a strong way, you know, and they just happen to be there."

Wonderful! And the rest of it?

"Good! Very good!"

You imagined yourself singing well and walking off feeling happy?

"Yes. Yes. And then I did a little visualization of whatever last night was going to be, and I got the index cards and I made all kinds of funny designs. Is that good?"

That's really good!

"Each one has its own character that kind of reflects the piece. Then I wrote my words on it. So now I can sort of visualize the card itself."

Perfect!

"So, on the way to the audition, I ran into some friends on the train. They were going too. I showed them my index cards. They thought that was great."

We both laughed.

"So I sang. I was tired, but I still thought that I sang pretty well. And I was able to keep my concentration. The only thing I noticed in the first piece was, whenever I would start to get a little unsure of myself, I'd start looking at the floor. I just don't think that's a good idea."

You mean while you're actually singing?

"Yeah. Whenever I was unsure of myself, either vocally or with what the character was doing, I would just lower my eyes a little bit, and I don't want to do that."

What would you rather do?

"Well, I don't know. I think I should look straight out. Because if you're looking at the floor, the audience can't see you. I don't know if it really takes away from the performance, but I noticed that I did it every time I was feeling a little insecure about something."

How many times was that?

"Four."

During one piece?

"Yeah."

Was that during the Rossini?

"Yes. I think it came more from what the character would be thinking about, rather than vocal problems. I may have to do some work on that. And then the second piece they asked for was the Bernstein."

Good!

We both laughed.

I called them and I told them to do that.

"You did?!" She laughed harder. "But I was kind of surprised. I thought they would ask for *Carmen*, but you never know. I remembered my words, luckily, and took time to take a couple of breaths."

Great.

"And I can just say, even though I was tired, it was still

pretty good. So that was that. I didn't know what they thought of me, but I don't particularly care."

What did you think about your performance?

"I thought I was good!"

When you did the Bernstein piece, did you use 'vowels' and 'flow'?

"Yeah, in a lot of places. There was one place I didn't. But I started out doing that."

Do you feel it got you off to a good start?

"Yes. Definitely. And I remember one part, just before there's a kind of crazy middle section where you have to sing a lot of high notes, I just kept calming myself down because you have to be very calm before you sing that. And it worked."

How'd you do that?

"I think I thought of just taking control of the tempo and calming it down, so that I would be in a place where I would be ready to sing it."

I like that. How are the 'what ifs' doing?

"Oh, God! I don't know. . . . I'm really just pushing them aside, but it's hard, because in some ways you can take comfort in hearing them and it's very hard to push them away. But I keep doing it."

Why is there comfort in what they have to say?

"I don't know. After last night's audition, I thought, 'Gee, that was pretty good.' And I thought, 'Why aren't these people just jumping up and down for joy that they were able to hear me sing?' But they weren't jumping up and down. They were like, 'Oh great, great. Nice. Okay, good.' I think they should be jumping up and down for joy, and they just weren't doing that. And so I thought, 'Well, am I crazy?' I must be crazy!"

Well, you're certainly not, but you have no control over anyone else's responses. How do you know they didn't have a fight with their spouses that morning or that their houses hadn't gone into foreclosure?

"Oh, yeah. I see what you mean."

Don't take it personally. It probably had nothing to do with you, and trying to control it is a waste of time and energy and distracts you out of your center. They may not like your hair. Maybe they were looking for a blonde. And that has nothing to do with you.

"I guess not."

Things that are under our control make us feel more comfortable and secure. Trying to control things that are out of our control make us nervous. So pay attention to the things you can control, like your breathing, self-talk, your cue words and focus. Take care of those things and let go of the things that are out of your control. Do you agree with that?

"Right!"

Others' responses to you or your singing or what your character is supposed to be doing are somewhat out of your control. I shouldn't say out of your control, but not under your total control.

"Right. I can't make them like me."

No. That's exactly it. All you can do is do your best.

"Ohhhhh!"

I'm sorry, but this is reality. You need to accept that. All you can do is go in there and do your best.

"That's kind of a relief, in a way."

It's just like critics. You really can't control what they say. Can you accept that?

"I think I have to. Because I always think, 'What if I sing my best? Then everybody will know how great I am.' But I've never sung my best, really."

So back to the 'what ifs.' I'm still wondering why they're still comforting to you. I guess they'll be going to Chicago with you.

"Oh God! I don't want them to come to Chicago with me!"

Well, they're going to go. They've already booked the flight. They might be sitting in first class.

"Right!" More laughter.

How's your unwavering confidence doing?

"Oh, God! Oh, God!" She laughed. "That was exhausting, very hard. But I did it for most of the day yesterday and then I had it when I got back from the audition."

Keep that up.

"Saturday I fly in and meet with them and talk with them and then Sunday morning I sing. On Saturday I'll have a coaching, but not any kind of audition."

Who coaches you?

"Whoever will be playing the piano for me on Sunday. One of their staff."

Just so you can get in synch?

"Yeah. Talk about whatever things the piece has."

After that, you may want to update your process cues. And then, when you get back to your hotel room, mentally rehearse your Centering and performance, using those cues. Oh, you should also change the index cards.

"Oh . . . [laughs] . . . but they're so pretty."

Make more pretty ones.

"Okay."

Let see, what else. Back to your eyes. Is the Centering working? Are you pleased with the breathing?

"I am, I am."

Was it nine or ten breaths before you went on?

"Oh no. I did about five."

And five got you there?

"Yeah. Well, maybe it didn't really get me there, but I felt like I was ready to sing."

What do you mean by not really there?

"I don't know." She laughed. "I was breathing, but I didn't have my mind on it like I had before."

But that's the whole idea, to get your mind on it. Don't just go through the motions. It's supposed to capture your attention on one thing in the middle of a storm swirling around you. You should feel like you're at the eye of the storm. It should be relatively calm there, in spite of everything that's going on around you. You can take a break from that if you're not caught up in it. Just get back to being at your center. Take the time. In fact, give yourself extra time; you don't want to rush it.

"So be able to time it, because I'll know who goes before me."

That's right. It will work for you if you use it.

"I have a feeling that the minute I walk into the theater, I'll probably want to be starting that."

Allow yourself the time. Before you did the Bernstein piece, what did you do?

"I took three breaths. Is that enough?"

You tell me. Was it enough?

"I took one breath for each word and then one breath just to feel that I was at my center."

Were you?

"Yeah, I think I was."

And that set you up to start the piece well?

"Yeah. And I felt pretty grounded for that. But beforehand, it was kind of crazy. I have a habit of talking to people too much . . . "

And spinning out?

"Yup."

Let's go back to your third sequence of breaths. After you've gotten in touch with your center, you were going to breathe and say your cue words and then open your eyes and project that energy out to a point. Did you find a point?

"You know, I didn't." She laughed. "So, to a specific place?"

Imagine standing where you're going to be singing, so you can figure out the best place to direct that energy.

"All right, got it."

Now imagine tacking your index cards up right there.

"I think you lost me."

Before you go in to sing, when nothing's going on, find the place where you'll be standing.

"You mean, actually, physically go out on stage?"

Yes. And as you're standing there, look out and find a place on the wall or a curtain out in the theater, wherever your voice would best go. Once you find that, imagine tacking up your index cards and then projecting your voice out there.

"I see, out to that place."

And then, when you do go on stage to sing, there are your cards. And rather than looking at the floor—look at the cards.

"Great! I'll have a place to go."

A place that will remind you of what you want to do. And with your new, fancy cards, it's a friendly place. The floor can't offer that.

"I don't know why I look at the floor. I don't do that when I'm performing. I only do that in auditions."

So when you're doing your mental rehearsals for the audition, imagine directing your focus out there. It will look a lot better to those watching.

"Great. I'm all excited now!"

So you're all set.

"I am?"

Yeah. But . . . you're not perfect.

"No."

And you're probably not going to sing perfectly. I just want you to do what you've been doing. That's all you need to do, Veronica. Just remember that you've prepared and when you do step on stage, you'll be ready. All you have to do then is do what you've been practicing and rehearsing, and you'll be fine.

"Okay. I believe it."

Good. Good. You've made some incredibly wonderful strides.

"Yeah. This has been great."

And you're going to be nervous, but you've got ways to deal with it. You've got a great strategy designed to get you centered, not worrying about outside things or other people. Continually go there, do your breathing and remember your cue words. Don't just go through the motions. Really hold on to them, get their value and then project that energy out to your cards. Basically, we've got a big feedback loop between you, your center and your cards, which brings you back to your cue words inside you.

"Aha!"

And it's just you and you and you. Within that big loop or circle, you can do just fine; and you will.

"Okay, that's very easy to picture. I can't wait to go try it! I want to do it now and get it over with!"

We both laughed.

So if you have some time today, continue to go through some situations and shuffle the cards and then practice putting the card out there and, if you get into any difficult spots in any of the pieces, simply find your cards. In fact, for today, if you're going to do it at home, I would literally find a far wall and—

"Stick them up there?"

Yes!

"Yeah, that's what I'll do."

Okay! I'm proud of you. You're doing great!

"Oh, thank you. I'm so excited. I can't wait to try it."

So say 'hi' to the 'what ifs' on the plane. Go up to first class and visit them.

"Oh, I will. I'm going to give them a copy of my cards to enjoy."

We both laughed.

Wow, Veronica was discovering things about herself that she probably never expected to learn. Who would have thought that the "what ifs" that plagued her mental confidence for so long would become a comfort to her? But this realization was not only understandable — it was expected. By embracing them as part of an audition, Veronica could actively involve them in the entire process of building courage, singing with confidence, and using the high energy to do her best. The rest of Veronica's final preparation involved some fine-tuning of last minute problems — using a focal point to center upon, and keeping her eyes up and focused throughout the entire performance. As for Brian, he was working through similar preaudition butterflies, and we discussed his final practice routines and last minutes jitters.

NORMAL FEARS AND DOUBTS

I heard from Brian a week later.

How's it going?

"Really good. Yesterday was my last big day at work. I played a good audition for another friend; he put me through my paces very quickly. He's one of the better players in the band, so he made me a little nervous. Other times I would have lost a little focus, but not this time. He pointed out some different technical things, so each time I do this, I get a little something extra."

Great!

"But I figured that would be the last time I do that before Houston. I don't need to work on too many things at once. I find that I end up working on nothing or try to do too many things. The brain can only do one thing at a time, basically. So I have all my process cues written out, and they are just how I'm going to start it. I know how the piece starts and then I have rhythmic subdivisions, and for some of them I have what happens just beforehand. I think of that and I think in the rhythm. Like for the Beethoven *Eroica* trio, the first phrase starts after a gear shift of tempo, and that sometimes throws me off. So I decided I'm just going to take it where I know the tempo ought to be and then transfer that to the beginning. That works pretty well for me."

Good!

"I spent about four hours practicing yesterday, including the session with my friend. So now I think I need to taper off."

Let me explain something in athletic terms. Let's take springboard divers who've been practicing their eleven competition dives over and over again. Early and midway through the season, they will do each dive three or four times, then move on to the next dive in sequence and do that one three or four times. As they get closer to the competition though, they start doing what are called 'lists.' They do only one of each dive and then move on to the next dive, the same as they'll be doing in the competition. When they're cutting back, or 'tapering' this way, it frees up some time. They can use that extra time to do mental preparation and mental rehearsal, and back off on the physical repetitions. So I would say the same for you. Have short run-throughs of the excerpts. Turn on the tape recorder, go through your preparation and Centering, come in and play forty-five seconds of first the random pick, and then pick the next excerpt. Try to do ten or fifteen pieces like this.

"So turn the tape deck on, go out, come back in and play a random list. Just 'one-time-only practicing' as I would to call it."

Yes, and after ten or fifteen minutes, stop and go on to something else and come back to it later.

"So I should still do a few of those before Houston. See, I don't want the effort to get stale."

This will keep it from becoming stale.

"Am I still practicing the process cues?"

You're still using the 'Post-it' phrases with the beginning of the pieces. You're rehearsing that process?

"Yeah, that takes the emphasis off, 'Oh no, here's this one!' A lot of them are very positive. Most of the ones I played for my friend were like, 'All right, let's do this!' and, 'Yeah, I'm ready to go with this one.' That's a good sign to me."

That's a great sign.

"But he did find a few things at fault and had some comments."

That's fine.

"Yeah, that was good. He wasn't sure how much to nail me, but I was thinking that this is what I need, because they're going to do the same thing in Houston. What should I do about Sunday? My flight gets in there about two in the afternoon. I'll be playing around ten-thirty, Monday morning."

I wouldn't do a whole lot of practicing on Sunday.

"I was planning on taking most of the day off."

Good!

"Just do a little bit of playing."

And get yourself acclimated, obviously drink a lot of water, walk around, shake it out, stay loose.

"Yeah, I'm going to drink on the plane. I mean water!"

And if you do have any nervous thoughts, just remember all the work that you've done. And it's all done!

"Yeah, I had some of those today. After the rehearsal, I started having my first preaudition anxious feelings."

Ah. Normal fears and doubts.

"Yeah, I've got them."

Well then, just say, 'Hi. I'm glad to see you again, but this time I'm prepared.'

"My old friend. I guess I still have some work to do. I wish I had a little more time, but I think I always think that when I come to an audition."

Even if you had another six months, Brian, at the end of that time you'd still probably want another couple weeks.

"Probably!"

I know with race car drivers, they're always going over the track one more time and refining the points where they're going to shift and brake and where they can pass. I was eating supper with one of the drivers the night before the Miami Grand Prix, and he said: 'What should I do tonight? Should I go over the track one more time?' I told him that he was as prepared as he was going to get, and that the best thing for him to do was to relax, knowing that when the flag went down in the morning, he'd be ready. I'll say the same thing to you. You're ready.

"Yeah, I mean, I'm pretty ready. My chops are in great shape and my brain has never been in better shape, thanks to you. So Sunday night, just know that I'm ready and kick back?"

And if you have a 'what if,' think, 'No, I've done my preparation,' and see yourself going through the Centering, using the process cues and then nailing it.

"And then Monday just get up, warm up, and walk in and do it."

Do what you've been rehearsing.

"Do you want me to call you on Sunday?"

I'm not sure if I'm going to be home. But I would just tell you to have fun and remind you to do what you've been doing. The goal is not to try to play perfectly, but to play optimally, the best you can, given the extreme circumstances. This is not the time to try for a peak experience. The goal is not to play over your head or try to reproduce the absolute best you've ever done in your whole life. Just play the way you've been practicing and playing recently.

"I need to give myself permission to play like Brian."

Please don't try to do anything else, because you haven't practiced that.

"Yeah, play like me. My goal is to go out there and lay it down for them and play like I know I can. And they'll like it."

And that's all you can do, Brian. No extra pressure.

"I hope not! I think if I do that, they will like it. So just know that I'm ready and kick back and get used to the place, relax, and maybe do a little more visualization."

And if you do feel any anxiety, just do a quick visualization of seeing yourself nailing this piece or playing that excerpt well.

"So be prepared for my old friend. Do you think that might happen?"

Do I think he'll be there? He wouldn't miss it! But you know what to do.

"Yeah. Just counter the negative with 'This time, it's going to be like this,' and remind myself that this is how I can play if

I just allow myself. All right. So I have a little bit of time tonight and then I've got most of the day tomorrow and then I leave."

Can you try to call me after you get into Houston?

"Yeah, the flight gets in around two."

Sounds like you're ready, Brian. You just need to do what you've been doing.

"Maybe some more visualization. I've been seeing myself walking into the musician's entrance door, signing in, and just chilling out and focusing. And when they knock on the door, I just get my horn and walk in. I know the feeling very well. So I walk in—they usually give you the instructions—they say, 'Don't talk to the committee, blah blah blah.' I've done this enough times. And then I imagine walking out into the big hall and sitting down and getting myself centered and ready, looking at the excerpt and having this feeling of 'I know how to do this,' and then nailing it. How's that sound?"

Great! And if, in the middle, you feel anything, just take one or two Centering breaths and get your focus back and then continue.

"With the last run through with my friend, even though I wasn't particularly nervous, a couple of notes shook. I was trying to stay relaxed, but I was probably not as relaxed as I should have been. That's a sure sign that I've got too much tension, especially on some of the low notes."

So maybe take a little time after you get there and put some pressure on yourself to play some difficult low notes and then get centered before you go for it.

"So that still works. You see, I was going to taper off on practicing."

I'm just asking you to do some fine tuning with those notes.

"Okay, just a little bit. All right, so I'll do a little fine tune practice with my steady low notes. I figure with the concerts tonight and tomorrow, my chops will be ready for a break on Sunday. But a little fine-tuning certainly isn't going to hurt, especially down low, it's not going to blow them out. Okay, so I will give you a call probably Sunday evening. I will work on this stuff."

I look forward to talking with you then. Brian, I want you to know that you're ready. You're at an optimal level.

"Yeah, I'm about as ready as I'm going to be. You know, everything I've learned preparing for this audition I can put into use for my regular playing as well.

Brian's methodical personality had been an enormous benefit to him during this entire preparation, to the degree that he risked overpreparation! He was evidently confident enough in each excerpt to discontinue full practice session, and he agreed to let up a bit. But like Veronica, a few last minute problems continued to nag at him, and the centered breathing was reasserting its value in helping him take control over those weaker low notes. As for both of them, it was wonderful to see everything coming together. They were both capable of performing at their optimal levels, and we all knew it.

CHAPTER NINE

On Location

BACK TO THE HUB

Veronica and Brian had arrived at their respective auditions, and I was interested to hear how they were doing in their unfamiliar surroundings. Unfortunately, I never got a chance to speak to Brian before the audition, receiving only a brief message on my answering machine from a confident, self-assured Brian. Luckily, Veronica and I found time to chat that afternoon.

Hi! How's Chicago?

"Ohhhh, pretty scary!"

Did you get some sleep last night?

"Nope. I tried. I tried."

I'm sorry.

"I think I will tonight."

Good.

"It was a long day. I was very scattered. I met with the pianist and did the coaching. I didn't prepare very well for the coaching. I mean, in my mind. And so I didn't do what I wanted to do with my pieces, but I figure that's okay, because I will tomorrow."

There you go!

"It was just a long day and I'm tired. I figure I'd just go through the whole process. I know exactly how the process is going to go. I don't know exactly what pieces they're going to pick, but I figured I'd go through it in my mind before I go to bed and then get ready in the morning and go do it."

So are you nervous enough?

"I don't think I'm that nervous right now. Now that I'm here and it's inevitably going to happen, I certainly want to sing well. I really want to get enough rest so that my voice feels fresh. I want to be in control and do what I want to do."

Oh good!

"I really do! I think I get a little nervous, even though I don't feel it. I don't want to say hysterical; it's not quite that much. It's just a little scattered, I guess, so it's difficult to just focus on what I have to do because a million other thoughts come into my mind."

Then get back to the hub and focus on what you need to do, which is get centered and sing well.

"Yeah, in my new dress."

We both laughed.

That's it, in your new dress.

"That's what I need. I didn't have my dress on today!" We both laughed. "Ohhhhhhhhh gosh! And it's really unnerving to just fly in early in the morning and then have to be all fresh in the afternoon and be in a strange hotel. It's tough to stay positive."

But that's your job. You've got to fight for it.

"Exactly."

And for your unalterable, unwavering confidence?

"That's it!"

Please use everything you've rehearsed. And put the index cards up in your mind and use all the stuff we've discussed. It will work very well for you.

"Yeah. I think that the index cards are going to be pretty crucial because one of the heads of the program said, 'Well, you're going to walk out on that stage and you're going to look out into the audience and that theater is so huge, it's going to look like the jaws of hell.' Argh!"

We both laughed.

You'll just see your index cards. Everybody else can see the jaws of hell.

We both laughed.

"I'll make my index cards really big."

Good.

"I really think today was the hardest day, just coming in and seeing people. And then tomorrow, I just need to do my thing. That's really what I'm ready to do."

So I think you're a little bit nervous, and that's fine, because you're ready.

"Well, I'm excited to do it. I really am."

Just make sure you wear your new dress.

"Okay!"

We both laughed.

Well, that's it.

"Ready to go."

I'll try to call you. I want to hear the good news.

As Veronica pointed out, the arrival day can often be more pressure-packed than the day of the audition! Being surrounded by strangers, with the stress of travel, the unfamiliarity of the hotel, and the chaos at the audition can erase all of that comfortable familiarity you built up over time, unless you *fight* against it. Veronica realized this immediately and focused her attention on the audition, blocking out all other distractions. By now, her ability to stay positive was her biggest asset, and she looked ahead to the next day with excitement and courage. As for Brian, I could only wait to hear.

CHAPTER TEN

New Things

THE DRESS

Twenty four hours later I got a call from Veronica.

"It was great! It was great! I got the job!"

Congratulations!

"I got it. I'm in shock!" She laughed. "I keep on looking at the contract and making sure it's my name, because I can't believe it."

Oh, you turkey.

"I know." She laughed. "So it was a good day. I got some good sleep last night and I got up and took my time and then got ready and put on my dress. Oh, I had the weirdest dream though. I had a dream that I got to the audition and I took off my coat . . . and I . . . I . . . I didn't . . . I had a different dress on . . . I had the wrong dress on." She laughed.

An anxiety dream.

"Yeah. It was really good. Then someone had to give me another dress and it wasn't quite right, and I didn't have time to warm up. When I woke up I was very relieved that I still had a chance to go to the audition." She laughed. "So I went in and sang and I did what I wanted to do."

Which pieces did you sing?

"I sang the lighter Rossini first and then I walked off. They heard everybody and then they had me come back to sing a second piece. They asked for the Bernstein. It was good though, because I really started being chatty with people before, and then I walked off to the side and went through my Centering, like three times."

Good, good.

" . . . and then I went out and did it. But I tell you, this afternoon at the reception, just waiting to find out, was ten times more stressful than the singing. They had us all in this room and they made us wait an hour before they announced who they would be taking into the program. But I was standing there and they announced my name."

Congratulations! That's wonderful.

"Thanks. I really was able to do what I wanted. I took those breaths. And I thought of the cue words and I looked up and the theater was not the jaws of hell—it was really very nice, actually—and it really made all the difference, because I was in control. And I took as much time as I wanted. It became a really powerful thing to just say, 'I am out here now, this is my time.' It felt great."

Veronica, that's a huge step forward.

"So it really helped me and I was able, in a very stressful situation, to be nice to myself about it."

Hey! Another big step!

"Oh. Unheard of."

Did you put the index cards up?

"Yes, I did. What happened was, I made a big card last night before I went to bed. I was getting really scared and I made an index card that just said 'Courage!!!' on it with exclamation points. Because sometimes the cards started making me nervous. So I just made this one."

Be Courageous.

"And I think that was the card I was looking at, because I said, 'You can't lose if you're being courageous.' And anytime I would feel myself getting nervous, I just fought for it. I fought for having enough breath and fought for really, really doing it."

I'm so proud of you!

"Oh, God!"

You did it, Veronica.

"I did it. And I can't believe it. I can't believe it." She laughed. "Maybe it was the dress though, and not me."

I want a picture of you in that dress.

"Me in my winning dress? Okay, I would be thrilled."

Thanks.

"No, thank you. It really made all the difference in the world for me to be in control of an audition for once. I know I've still got a lot to work on, of course, but this is a big job. This is the biggest thing I've ever gotten, and it was so important. I can't believe it. So this is work for a year."

This is a year contract?

"Yeah. I have to move back here in March. It's a little scary, but it's okay."

Hey, no worry, you've got courage.

"Exactly. I've got that index card."

You can take that to Chicago with you.

"I think so. Hey, it's starting to hit me—I've got a job for the next year! Wow! This really made all the difference. It really moved me up to a different level of singing. Because the other singers there were really very good. You just had to have something else."

Well, you do. Maybe we can talk in a few days, after you come down. Congratulations. I'm very proud of you.

"Thank you, thank you."

THE NEW HORN

Twenty-four hours later, I got a message from Brian.

"Hey, Don. I tried to leave word with you yesterday, but your answering machine said you were out of town, so I guess I'll just have to leave this on your machine. I think you'll be happy to know that I'm the new second horn of the Houston Symphony. [Cheers and clapping in the background.] I'm very pleased about that and I think you'll be also. I would love to talk to you. I'll be here until Sunday, so please give me a call when you can and I'll give you all the details. It still hasn't sunk in yet. Hope to talk to you soon. Thanks. Bye bye."

So is this the happy ending to the story? More like a strong beginning to many future optimal performances for both Veronica and Brian! Through hard work, commitment, and focus, they had finally beaten the things that had held them back in their careers. Not only did they achieve what they set out to accomplish—success in major, career-making auditions—

they also gained a greater sense of confidence and optimism that was previously lacking. Veronica and Brian had learned that Centering and focusing are as important as correctly singing or playing the toughest passage in the next Bach aria or Hayden sonata. From now on, they could take their individualized programs with them to every future audition and important performance. This mental preparedness would always be with them, whether or not I was on the other end of the phone line. In fact, Veronica had several auditions coming up.

CHAPTER ELEVEN

Other Energy

IT JUST KICKED IN

Veronica had pulled it all together and wowed them in Chicago, but as with most people, not everything would always be so cut and dry. As I suspected, she had another audition lined up a week later, and for the first time, Veronica was exhausted. Suddenly, she was struggling with the flip side of energy control. Instead of having to focus excess energy, she was in desperate need of revving up! She called me immediately, at a total loss of what to do. I asked her how she was doing.

"Ahh, okay. I'm so used to having this high energy problem and trying to calm myself down. I'm having the opposite problem now. I have this audition tomorrow and I'm like, 'What am I doing. I'm too tired. I can't get up for it. And they won't want to give you a job anyway. And you're just the same as last year. You can work as hard as you want, but you're still not good'. Oh, I know who those voices are, but I told them to go away." She laughed.

And they didn't go away?

"No, they didn't go away! Oh, God! And I had to learn this brand new piece. The audition was supposed to be yesterday and I found out the night before that it was the next day, and I had to learn a new piece. It's basically singing a nursery rhyme. It's really not much harder than that. But it still requires the same amount of concentration and commitment if you're going to get up and sing anything, even if it's a scale, in front of people."

Okay.

"I know this is a lot of little things. So I learned the new piece and I went through it and made an index card for it. This is my best index card yet! I love it. It's the sweetest looking thing because it's a very funny little song. And it's so cute, it makes me happy."

Great!

"But sometimes I look at the card and I walk away and think, 'Well, the card's good but I'm not.' I just think that I should just walk into the audition and give them the card."

We both laughed.

Good idea.

"Yeah, really. I'm feeling so lethargic about this next audition. I'm just down about it."

What's it for?

"It's for the Orchestra of St. Luke's. They do a children's opera every year in October and November. It's pretty good money and the timing's really good. It's a good orchestra and it seems like I'd be just right for it. A friend called and said they were having callbacks this week. They weren't happy with the mezzos they had heard and asked her about me. So I already know, going in, that they don't even really like the people that have callbacks, and if I look at it objectively, I would be great, but I can't. Some part of me has to say, 'No. It's wrong for me to believe that I would be right for it.' I don't know."

Would you like it?

"Yeah, I would. But I just can't seem to get up for it."

Well, you ran your activation engine at a high rev rate for a long time.

"Yeah!"

You burned a lot of fuel and now you're feeling low energy. You and I have worked mainly on controlling the energy that's been too high. You did a good job with that. Now it's time to come at it from a point of low energy. You're not always going to have high energy, but that shouldn't stop you from singing well. Sometimes your engine's going to be slowed down.

"But I want it to be in a positive place, like I was in Chicago. That was a really great place; I was so excited and couldn't wait to sing."

But you can still sing well, even though you're not feeling tons of energy. You've got to realize that your good singing is somewhat independent of your energy levels. You can do it with a lot of adrenaline; you can do it when you're not up that much; you can do it when you're tired. The essential thing is that you can do it from wherever you are, as long as you're centered.

"Right. I know I can. I just have to trust that a little more."

Yes, but it's just more challenging to do when you're feeling low energy.

"You know, I'll be okay. I know I can get through the night."

And in the meantime, let your energy be low. You don't need to be up until you get there. And when you do, you're going to experience normal fears and doubts. Your activation level will go up and that will bring you to a different place. The essential thing is to focus on doing your best, which comes from being centered and performing from inside-out.

"Yeah, Okay. Well I did it this morning after breakfast. I was like, 'I'm just too tired to sing. I can't practice', but I did just that. I did some breathing and Centering, and then started practicing and it worked, even though I was not really feeling that great. You just have to be a little more concentrated about it. And it came out fine. I got some good work done. But it was exhausting."

I figured that inevitably, some of that high energy would burn off and you would drop below the curve.

"Oh, God! It's been terrible, terrible. I wish I could keep that energy up all the time."

You can't. You just can't.

"No, I can't. And then I give myself a hard time because I can't understand what's wrong."

So get some rest today, let the adrenaline kick in tonight, sing your best and then get some more rest.

"All right."

Maybe we can talk over the weekend or sometime next week.

"Oh, good."

Please keep the same routine before you go in. Go through the process.

"Okay. Thanks, Don. I'll let call you and let you know how it went."

That sounds good, Veronica. I'll talk to you then.

After months of getting control over her high energy, Veronica now had to realize that the same principles of Centering and focusing apply to building energy from the ground up. This is a fundamental of mental preparedness—to have the ability to be in complete control of your own energy levels and mental states. Whether Veronica needed to calm herself down or rev herself up, both involved the channeling of energy from deep within her body and mind, and out through her voice. With her newfound confidence and index cards, Veronica was more than ready for this next hurdle. I got her call the next day.

How did it go?

"I just got the phone call."

Well . . . ?

"Well . . . there was a message on my machine and I just called them back and they gave me the details. So, exactly what you said would happen, happened. The energy was there—it just kicked in and I actually had to calm myself down. They were very nice and I was in control and it was fun. And I left there feeling like if I don't get the job, it has nothing to do with me, because I was really great. But I got it!"

That's wonderful. Congratulations!

"Oh, thank you. And thanks for talking to me yesterday. That really helped."

You're welcome.

Bye bye.

Epilogue

On his way to Houston, Brian had stopped in Lake George to visit. We went to a park where we spent the afternoon working with peak performance skills and trying different ways to affect flow states in his playing. It's a quantum difference from optimal to peak performance and not easy to generate at will. We learned that an essential skill for him was that of letting go. I asked him to play more freely, without concern for missing notes. I even suggested he play some "clams" on purpose. He didn't like the exercise.

We tried a number of things in the park, like painting pictures with his sound and playing around casually with different kinds of music, such as Irish folk tunes. I'm not exactly sure what eventually turned the key that afternoon, but he finally got "there," and we both heard it immediately. It was indescribable! Getting there more often would become a priority after he got settled in Houston. In the meantime, I would be spending the next week with the Lake George Opera.

In the years since then, Veronica and Brian have found new trust in themselves and in their ability to perform well under pressure. But they also carry within them a deeper awareness that reaches beyond artistic or musical prowess—a deepseated knowledge that they can approach any challenge that comes their way with the same commitment, focus, and self-confidence that we built together.

Veronica is back in New York, following many successes in Chicago. Brian is still with the Houston Symphony. Remember Ed from the golf course? He is still the Principal Bass with the Syracuse Symphony and he's still playing golf. His handicap has come down several strokes and he won his club championship a number of times. Isn't that wonderful.

I have continued working with performing artists and a variety projects. For the past four years, I have taught at The Juilliard School and the New World Symphony, and have conducted master classes at Yale, Northwestern, Manhattan, Oberlin, Michigan, Curtis, the Aspen Music Festival, the OperaWorks Intensive Program, and the Perlman Music Program. My students continue doing well in competitions and auditions. I still get very moved when one of them wins.

Last year, I completed the interactive form of the Artist's Survey and made it available online at *www.Dongreene.com*. Now a performing artist can receive an individualized profile and recommended success program immediately after completing the survey. I recently finished *Performance Success*, as a sequel, due to be released later this year.

But more importantly, what about you? Have you started to realize your dreams? Are you ready to begin the process? If you think this approach can work for you, grab a few index cards and learn how to Center. Develop your routine and do some simulation training. Keep raising the bar. Under increasing pressure, practice summoning up your courage, trusting yourself, and going for it! As I'm sure you realize, there's nothing as exciting and powerful as giving it your very best.

Centering Instructions

Step 1: Form A Clear Intention

What you intend to accomplish when you come out of the Centering. "I am going to. . . ."

Step 2: Pick A Focus Point

Select an external point lower than eye level before closing your eyes.

Step 3: Start Abdominal Breathing

Breathe slowly and deeply into your lower stomach (3 to 7 breaths).

Step 4: Scan for Muscle Tension

Check your key muscles one at a time, then breathe out tension (3 to 7 breaths).

Step 5: Be at Your Center

Focus down to your center (3 to 7 breaths).

Step 6: Repeat Your Process Cue

Say it until you are in your right brain: seeing it, feeling it, hearing it (3 to 7 breaths).

Step 7: Direct Your Energy to Your Point

Let the energy flow from your center to your focus point. Go for it!

When you start practicing centering, it should take you between 15 and 45 breaths, which will take 30 seconds to 3 minutes. As with any learned skill, your ability to center will improve with correct practice and repetition. Start out by practicing centering three to seven times a day. If you use it as part of your normal routine, before you warm up, rehearse, or perform, you will soon notice positive effects. Eventually, you will be able to center in one to three breaths, that is, in 10 seconds or less.

When you start practicing, though, the goal is not to see how fast you can do it, but to accomplish the task of each step in the Centering process. Make sure that you first form a clear intention and pick a focus point, then start proper breathing before scanning your key muscles for tension. Take as many breaths as you need to get relatively relaxed and find your center before repeating your process cue and switching to your right brain. Then reconnect with your center and allow the energy to rise up from there, through the center of your body, up, and out to your point. Trust your talent and training so you can smile and courageously go for it!

You will soon experience that Centering will take you from a suboptimal state of tight muscles and overthinking to one that is much more suited for optimal performance. The more you become familiar with that place, the easier and quicker it will be to get there. By the end of a week's practice, you should be Centering much better and starting to realize significant results.